PILGRIMAGE WITH FISH

PILGRIMAGE WITH FISH

A fishing memoir

by

Ed Moses

n
RIVERS
e
PRESS
W
MSUM

© 2004 by Ed Moses
First Edition
Library of Congress Control Number: 2003112681
ISBN: 0-89823-222-8
Cover design, photo illustration, and interior designed by Kim Morales.
Author photo by Keith Vanderlin.

The publication of *Pilgrimage with Fish* has been made possible by the generous support
of Janis LeClaire and other contributing members of New Rivers Press.

For academic permission please contact Frederick T. Courtright at 570-839-7477 or
permdude@eclipse.net. For all other permissions, contact The Copyright Clearance Center
at 978-750-8400 or info@copyright.com.

New Rivers Press is a nonprofit literary press associated with
Minnesota State University Moorhead.

Wayne Gudmundson, Director
Alan Davis, Senior Editor
Donna Carlson, Managing Editor
    Honors Apprentice: Rosanne Pfenning
    Pilgrimage with Fish Team: Jessie Johnson, Leslie Knudson
    Editorial Interns and Volunteers: Kris Benson, James Boobar, Jolly Foster Corley,
        Nichole Deconcini, Stephanie Gillen, Angela Glaser, Erik Hagen, Crystal Jensen,
        Jessie Johnson, Leslie Knudson, Brett Ortler, Michael Schlemper, Heather Steinmann,
        Andrea Tieman, Rebecca West
    Inventory Coordinator: Brett Ortler
    Marketing Coordinator: Abbey Thompsen
    Media Coordinator: Gerri Stowman
    Web Site Coordinator: Deb Morris
Allen Sheets, Design Manager
    Designers: Julie Campbell, Kim Morales, Jocie Suess, Erin Zellers
Nancy Edmunds Hanson, Promotions Manager
    Students: "Promotional Communications" and "Fundraising" classes
Marlane Sanderson, Business Manager

Printed in the United States of America

New Rivers Press
c/o MSUM
1104 7th Avenue South
Moorhead, MN 56563
www.newriverspress.com

For Jeremy

Good times on the water and more to come

CONTENTS

"Many men go fishing all their lives without knowing that it is not fish they are after."

-Henry David Thoreau

one

Launching

The subject is fish; the pursuit of fish. The subject is life. At some meta-level, it's all one.

Imagine yourself—for us lucky ones this is going to require some stretching—hungry. I'm not talking about mild midnight speculations as to the contents of the freezer. Rather, the real gut-growling, head-spinning, leg-wobbling thing—consuming today, worse tomorrow. The closest I've come was on an ill-planned backpacking trip, too wet to cook anything; what I had to eat was Power Bars the consistency of cold taffy. Most unwisely, I had not sampled one ahead of time. Nevertheless, though they would have yanked the two-thousand-dollar bridge right out of my mouth, I would have choked them down—if I'd been hungry enough. Before moving on to grubs and grasshoppers. Or, as I was hiking in Pennsylvania with its hundreds of miles of trout streams, I might have tried for a fish.

Imagine yourself, then, in straits more dire than mine, gazing speculatively about at the local insect life, but also at the water—ocean, lake, pond, river, creek. Maybe it's not hunger-right-now that's got you by the guts, but hunger next week or next winter. That would be good, a clear head being helpful in addressing the problem that now faces you: there are fish in that water, fish for today's dinner, fish you could salt, dry, freeze for hard times, or sell, or barter for (let's say) cornmeal, canvas, tools, and weapons. How do you propose to get them out?

By scooping with your bare hands, possibly, grizzly bear-fashion, if the fish are migrating salmon and the stream is small enough. Or you could dive right in after them, otter-fashion. Better be a strong swimmer, as humans can get themselves into terrible trouble in the water in no more than a minute or two. Beware, also, hypothermia if the water temperature is below seventy degrees Fahrenheit; you wouldn't want to get muddled and lose track of your limitations. Beware tides, undertows, and currents. The current in the gorge below Niagara Falls, in which nothing human can live, runs about twenty-five miles an hour. A waist-deep four-mile current, a mild-enough riffle in a Pennsylvania smallmouth river, will sweep you onto whatever lies below. Call it sandstone. Imagine careening into a jagged sandstone wall at a rapid walk.

All in all, then—unless you're wearing a wetsuit and scuba gear, but why in that case are you so hungry?—the water had better be warm and quiet; and clear, so you can see the fish, unless of course you prefer to try *noodling*. To noodle, wade at night into the edge of a murky midwestern or southern river, at a spot with undercut banks. Waist-to-chin-deep, poke blindly about among the tangled roots. Your objective here is to induce a fifty-pound flathead catfish to latch onto your hand, at which point you in turn can grab it by the lower jaw and wrestle it ashore. A significant blood-alcohol level is helpful. You're more likely to be struck by lightning than dragged under, trapped in the roots, drowned.

Assuming, however, that you've dived cold sober into water in which you can see fish, how are you going to capture them? With your bare hands? Here I can only report that my fishing son, in many swimming trips to a local trout/bass/carp stream, has not succeeded once. Remember also that the caloric energy yielded by the fish must significantly exceed the energy expended in catching it. So you'll need a weapon, such as a barbed spear. Also your quarry will need to be of a reasonable size—try spearing an eight-inch brook trout. Let's say that the fish is a ten-pound carp and that you have indeed speared it. It will yield about four pounds of edible flesh—using the term loosely, as a carp tastes like the bottom of a stagnant pond—and you can boil up the head for soup. It will keep you on your feet for quite some time.

Having discovered the concept of spearfishing, moreover, you'll come up with variations. Instead of swimming, you could wade (carp browse in the shallows, mornings and evenings). Or crouch on a rock above the water—so much for hypothermia. Like an Innuit of the old school at a seal hole, you could lurk by a hole in the ice—remembering that whereas the seal is drawn to the hole by its need to breathe, your fish will have to happen to swim within range. Or fish from a raft or a boat. Tie a line to your spear, and now you can throw instead of just jabbing. Your tribe has bows? Try an arrow. Gunpowder? From here it's but a step to that scoped 30.06 deer rifle. (Remember to allow for refraction.)

If you've got gunpowder, most likely you've got dynamite. Toss a stick of it into a pond, you've got fish—also, presumably, frogs,

3

salamanders, the odd duck. Given the legal and environmental implications, you might want to try this one a fair distance from home. The same with poison—rotenone in *your* pond?

You could try shocking them. It works for certain eels and catfish.

With a whole crowd of people to feed, the multiplying loaves and fishes a dim and distant memory, you could drain the pond entirely. Hack or blow a hole in the dam, set a net against the breach, let nature take its course. Should you have that same crowd to feed a year later, better pray for the Second Coming.

With an eye to a sustainable yield, then, consider a trap. A reed basket sunk in the Nile, let's say, its funnel-shaped mouth upstream; what swims into it stays, for fish are not as smart as people. Watch out for crocodiles. Crocodiles are not as smart as people either—would you care?

Or consider a net. Now, once you get the details worked out, you're really onto something. With a boat, a net, a big lake or an ocean, you can eat fish, freeze fish, and sell fish . . . with big enough nets you can damn near extinguish entire species. This is the Tragedy of the Commons: the family of the far-sighted conservationist, concerned for the good of all over the long term, goes hungry; the rest get that much richer in the short term; in the end, nothing changes.

Maybe, then, it would make more sense to use hooks—as in the swordfishing so vividly depicted in *The Perfect Storm*. Former sword captain Linda Greenlaw, in her own book *The Hungry Ocean*, claims that nothing that spawns (fish, she meant, as opposed to whales) can be fished down purely by hook and line. Though others disagree, I took her word for it and began ordering swordfish again; I love swordfish. I also love brook trout—and would have in particular on that hungry backpacking jaunt. Had I thought of packing a hook and line, I could in turn have looked at grubs and grasshoppers not as emergency protein sources but as bait. More than once I walked along streams with trout in them—I could see them, some upwards of six inches long. Like Nick Adams in Hemingway's classic "Big Two-Hearted River," I'd have tossed my hopper-baited hook into a dappled pool . . . and unlike Nick, this being life rather than fiction, most likely just sat there. Sat longer and a little longer yet, hungrier all the while.

Because between every approach to fishing heretofore mentioned, and fishing with hook and line, lies a divide the likes of the lower Amazon. For what do fish scooped from the water, stabbed, shot, dynamited, trapped, netted have in common? Simply that they happened to be in the wrong place at the wrong time. As opposed to the swordfish in the North Atlantic or the brook trout in the Pennsylvania creek, which *has to be persuaded to cooperate*. In plain language, tricked into biting. And while, at a minimum, some people are smarter than some fish on some days; while you might seem to have every possible advantage—fishing boat costing half the price of your house, crammed with fish-finding electronics adaptable to submarine warfare; reel crafted to tolerances that would shame next year's Mars launch; rod bearing the same relationship to your granddaddy's cane pole as, say, the Eiffel Tower to a scrubby creek-side willow; line invisible except in ultraviolet light, with the tensile strength of bridge cable; ultra-realistic artificial minnow from Finland resembling an artifact from the Museum of Modern Art; the accumulated lore of your ancestors, and the canniest guide in three states—still, this much is true: if you fish for longer than an hour, a day, a season, the time will come when you feel like a fool.

Trust me: you are going to be humbled.

5

Yet you must be doing this for pleasure. With a bow to subsistence fishermen everywhere, for sport. Why?

And stranger yet: picture, in the dawn of human time or perhaps somewhat later, the forenoon of human time, let's say, a man (because he had more leisure than the women) sitting on a riverbank. For no particular reason; it was a pleasant summer evening, and he held in his lap a pole with a line tied onto it, and onto that a hook. Of what material any of them were made we don't know, it doesn't matter, but presumably the hook was metal, for the man was settled and well-fed. He'd baited with a worm—what else? Maybe he was bottom-fishing, but I prefer to think of him as idly watching a bobber, which, at this stunningly significant historical moment, now goes under. He gives it a few seconds, then hauls the fish ashore. Actually, hauling is what you do to a laden net. He plays it out, then, lands it, it's a nice one, a variety that people eat and enjoy, or else what happens next doesn't count. Let's say it's a catfish, since catfish have been around forever and thrive everywhere. Dinner on the fin. Yet this fisherman unhooks it, gazes at it with . . . what? At least admiration, as something worth preserving, because . . . he now . . .

Throws it back.

And in that moment, everything changed. His evening beside the water was no longer about possession of fish, consumption of fish: want-a-fish, need-a-fish, care-not-how-I-come-by-that-fish. The success of his outing could no longer be measured in pounds. Evidently, perhaps to his own astonishment, his interest lay not in fish-in-themselves, but in some radical process involving fish. Fish not as food but as playmate? Soulmate? Totem, intimation of divinity, avatar of God? Naturally, when some unspeakable child hiding in the bushes tattled on him, everyone thought he was crazy.

Simple-minded at best. I can only hope that, like some of the North American Plains tribes, they respected him as a Holy Fool, left him to his peaceful evenings.

Everything began to change, I should have said. In earlier centuries and deep into the twentieth, catch-and-release prevailed mainly, I suspect, among those who owned the water—and thought of themselves therefore as owning what swam in it. As a child I fished once or twice in a lake owned by an uncle; one could keep rock bass, panfish of modest assessed worth, but had to restore the lordly largemouth. The lairds of Scottish salmon streams released their salmon; nightly their gamekeepers lay in wait for poachers, who knew what salmon were for. But on public waters? Waters, especially, far from home?

There were pioneers—the famed fly fisherman Lee Wulff, who in the thirties wrote, "A great game fish is too valuable to be caught only once." My ancestors were not among them.

Back in the twenties, in some Ontario lake, my grandfather caught a muskellunge—what you might think of as a fresh-water barracuda—which probably weighed over thirty pounds; still the mightiest catch in my family's history. He had no use for it, but kept it anyway—gave it to somebody who lived up there. With a fish that size, that was what you did. In the fifties, in a Minnesota lake we journeyed to each August from our home in Kansas, my mother caught a largemouth bass weighing over five pounds, a huge fish for that place. Naturally, though every day we caught more smaller fish than we could eat, we kept it. Baked it for supper; it tasted weedy.

All across Canada, meanwhile, from every lake and river with easy access, people were taking fish by the freezer-full. Northern pike, smallmouth bass, lake trout, and in particular, for their legendary texture and flavor, walleye—what could twenty or fifty or a hundred fish, a year's supply, possibly matter? What could it matter, even, if half of them never made it to the freezer? Fish, great strings of them, were for showing off on the dock. Only, for any given large lake, multiply by a few hundred or thousand. Multiply by the eggs that never got laid, and now, fifty years later, try taking your son or daughter to that lake for a fishing vacation. Not knowing the water, you can get skunked more days than not. Go out with a guide, and if the wind and pressure and clouds aren't just right, you can get as near to skunked as matters. The Province of Ontario, whose economic life's blood has thinned out right along with the walleye, now sells conservation licenses at a handsome discount. Catch-and-release, a little late, is the new Holy Grail. Should have thought of that fifty years ago.

Yet for all this, as the poet truly said, nature is never spent. Everything changes. In my early and middle years, I kept and cleaned more fish than I ever ate. As recently as last year, threw out a couple packages of freezer-burned weakfish. My fishing son Jeremy, ardent companion on the water, has not kept a single fish in his entire life. Jeremy is sixteen as I write this and knows how; we're not talking kid-fish here. Four-pound weakfish, flounder that had grown men drooling, catfish, walleye, trophy smallmouth—back home they go. Which is to say that we as a family—and, I think, we as a fishing race—have evolved. We're hungry for something too big to fit into a frying pan—but what? As somebody's Significant Other, the practical-minded Gathering Department of the Hunting-Gathering Team, has repeatedly asked: if you're not even going to bring the fish home, what's the point?

There is, in that sense, no point. What is the point of deep waters?

two
___

First Cast

The first cast of the day plops into the West Branch of the Susquehanna River shortly after six o'clock in the morning. It's mid-July, a few weeks past the Solstice; the sun has risen over the rim of the world, the outer world of commerce and the kids' breakfast to get before work. Here, though, the densely wooded far shore, some two hundred yards across the flat pool stretching out from the boat landing, lies shrouded in mist and mystery. We may not see the sun for an hour or more, and glad of it, for the day later will be hot.

The first cast is Jeremy's. I myself am fully engaged in urging the canoe toward midstream, not ten yards off the landing when I hear *whoosh* from the rod, *whir* from the line, then the lure splashing in; then, from the woods across the river, crows cawing. Water spilled along the paddle blade, and that is all. Nobody else around. It's Monday, a summer haven for students and teachers, and the water's low—just four-tenths of a foot above low water mark, according to the newspaper yesterday morning, falling slowly. Downstream where we're going, the powerboats can't get over the riffles. Our canoe, with us sloshing along beside it, can—go anywhere. It's a fifteen-foot aluminum Grumman, a lightweight weighing fifty-five pounds; turn it over, it looks like a persistent child worked it over with a hammer. There's no give to the riverbed sandstone. And yet, unlike many a costlier craft, it has never in over thirty years sprung the smallest leak. Ever since my old spinning rod got dragged into the bay off the Jersey coast, it's been the only object I own that I would truly mind losing. The other thing about low water is that it runs clear, green when the sun hits it, the bottom visible six or eight feet down; though here my paddle is still scraping, and Jeremy has thrown his lure back toward shore, into less water than that.

He's done it knowing what he's about. The lure itself is a prop bait, a torpedo-shaped two-and-a-half-inch-long plastic gizmo, green above and white below, with a propeller mounted in back. It's armed with two #4 Gamakatsu treble hooks, with which I've replaced the dull originals. (You test a fishhook by pressing it lightly against your thumbnail, then applying lateral pressure; if it digs in instead of sliding down, it's sharp.) One of us, as with every hook we've used for the last year or so, with a pair of long nosed pliers has pinched the barbs down. This lure, when retrieved with short, sharp jerks, thrashes in along the surface, imitating a dying minnow. You can cast it into a foot of water, as Jeremy has, without risk of snagging it on the bottom.

And in just about enough water to cover the dorsal fin is where a fish might be lying—a big smallmouth bass, up to twenty inches and four pounds, though most likely a good deal smaller. A twelve-inch fish weighing about a pound is a keeper, legally, theoretically, and in my fishing journal. Fourteen inches, a pound and a half or so, is average here in the West Branch. A whole lot of fuss over a fish the size of a kitten? But if you've seen a smallmouth bass rush at a school of minnows, you've seen speed and power that can make your hair stand up. The breaking strain of Jeremy's line is six pounds — six pounds dry out of the box, not counting knots, wear and tear, the vicissitudes of life — and if the drag on his reel should freeze up, snubbing that line up tight, a two-pound fish could snap it like a thread. Try breaking a four- or five-hundred-pound rope, no slack in it, by running from a standing start.

Smallmouth, the reference now open on my desk tells me, originally did not live east of the Appalachian Mountains. Someone put them in the water hereabouts over a hundred years ago, and they promptly went native. They're predators, feeding on minnows, frogs, crayfish, hellgrammites (the larval stage of the dobsonfly, resembling black jointed leeches with claws) — anything small enough to swallow. Sometimes called bronzebacks, they range in this river from dark brown to light greenish-tan. "Inch for inch and pound for pound, the gamest fish that swim," an old book claimed; freshwater fish that meant, as a little dabbling in the edge of the ocean has taught me. But we fish the waters given us to fish — home waters, with occasional excursions abroad — and how sweet and bountiful they are!

Jeremy gives his lure a twitch. Its rear-mounted propeller kicks up a flurry of water. Nothing comes to it, which is just as well. First-cast fish are too easy, set up expectations no day on this water can meet. Anyway, knowledge sustains us. In high season — mid-July through around mid-August — something always rises, sooner or later. Not like tourist-water, a lot of miles and a lot of dollars from home, where a blank initial hour can bring on existential unease, or dis-ease — is there anything down there? Is there, is there?

Ten years ago I was a tourist here, a ten-minute drive from my house. Then, when Jeremy and his twin brother were six, I began taking them out in the canoe, on the eight-mile downstream route we'll follow today. We saw fishing birds, kingfishers and great blue herons, in the air and along the shore, and carp in the water. One day Gregory and I passed a boat with two men in it, beside the boat a great splashing, then "Oh, no!" "What was it?" I hollered. "Muskie." Talk about restraint—that fish must have been close to four feet long. Talk about intimations. I hadn't fished since our first spring in Pennsylvania, 1983—tried the trout for a season, never caught any, got mightily tired of it. Not much more than whim, I think, got Keith, a friend, and me out on the West Branch with rods, as tourists. Keith, a native of these parts, thought we were fishing for chain pickerel, small relatives of northern pike. That was what he used to catch twenty-five or thirty years ago as a teenager, the last time he paid any attention to the river. Now here is a strange thing: there were, and are, no longer any pickerel in this water; or so few that seven years' fishing has not revealed one. What happened to them? I can only speculate based on what I do know: the water quality improved. Good environmental news is unfashionable, but there it is. Back in 1987 when I taught at Lock Haven University for a year, twenty miles or so upstream, the water there was too acidic from mine runoff to sustain fish. A couple of years ago the state fisheries people did a dive and spotted all sorts of fish—crappie, catfish, rock bass, most of all smallmouth. So what happened to the pickerel? The bass, a dominant, aggressive, top-of-the-food-chain predator, ate them. On that day of my first cast into the Susquehanna, Keith and I raised four bass, of which we caught none. We were tourists, but what even a tourist catches is what's in the water—three or four on a good day, up to fifteen or sixteen inches. Now, on a good day, it's more like eight or ten, and every season we see eighteen- to twenty-inch fish.

Jeremy, from the day of his first cast, was never a tourist. His brother fished at first, over the years drifted away from it; our swimming, picnicking, bird-watching trips together now offer a different kind of bounty. Keith might go down a time or two each summer, mostly guiding people, but he's found his true home on the ocean. Jeremy has stayed. One day when he was about ten he said to me, "What if I can't afford a boat when I grow up? What if I can't find the river?"

I said what you say. He'd inherit this boat. We'd put money aside in a special Jeremy Boat Fund, and the river wasn't going anywhere, anybody would know, just ask. And of course that got nowhere near the heart of it. What if it's not here anymore, the magic of it, the feeling I have right now? *What if I can't find my way home?*

Good question. "You can't go home again," people say, maybe because Thomas Wolfe said so most of a century ago. People grow up, things change. Move on.

Going home, if we're going to be literal-minded about it, would take me to the rocky bank of the Potomac River within the city limits of Washington, D.C. My father, stationed there during World War II, stayed on for a few years in the Civil Service. If you're a fisherman, if the water you can get to sustains piscine life in any form, you fish. I'm told I caught white perch, small ocean fish that ran up the river, when I was about three. No memory of it, so that was not in the true sense *first cast*. There were eels in that water, channel catfish, and herring which ran up in the spring. My father used to try snagging the herring—why I'm not sure except that they were fish, they were there—and here at last is an actual memory: one day he snagged a big catfish, over two feet long. He carried his tackle, spare hooks and sinkers and so on, in a small canvas backpack. A World War I relic it might have been, with, as we left the river, the fish's head and tail sticking out both sides. Though you could eat small catfish, this one, marinated for too long in that noxious soup, tasted like something fried in diesel oil. And a trip I was too young to be taken on: my father went upriver somewhere with a friend and came back late at night—but it was probably more like nine or ten—with *real fish,* rock bass and a smallmouth or two. Intimations from a world I'd not even imagined.

I've been told that people now catch big largemouth bass in the lower Potomac. That's lovely news, and I'm thinking that if some of the power players—why not even the Man himself?—were to wander down to the bank and throw in a line on occasion, they might come away with a new perspective on politics as usual. Myself, I won't be back. Memory's song is a distant humming, which might, after all, be wind, the white noise of any life.

Then in 1950, when I was six, my father landed a teaching job that took us to Manhattan, Kansas. Manhattan sits, or sprawls nowadays, near the confluence of the Blue and the Kaw River. Clearly its founders dreamed big dreams, but Manhattan turned out to lack the key geographical features that nourished its namesake—the Atlantic Ocean, to name just one—and so remained a modest college town. Fishermen take vacations from, not to, Kansas.

But there was the Blue, there was Lake Pottawatamie, and Wildcat Creek.

The Blue River, a prairie stream the size of this Susquehanna on which, with Jeremy's first cast still in the water, we're poised to begin our day's journeying, in the summer was never blue. Blue it must have been before the plows came, except sometimes below fords where bison herds churned up the bottom, or after heavy rain. When I knew it, though, it was nearly opaque, a pleasing milk chocolate color. We'd park at the top of a high bank, densely overgrown with sumac, wild black raspberry, anything tough enough to cling on; descend on a steep wooden staircase to a railroad bed halfway down, along which, during the June season, we'd walk and pick the raspberries. It was a fierce, sweaty, exhilarating scramble, above and below, with wasps to watch out for and catbirds calling; you'd emerge breathless onto the track, scratched and berry-stained, duck back into the brush sometimes out of the path of a freight train. But on fishing days we'd keep on down the second flight to the river.

An old concrete dam, twenty feet high or so with a derelict powerhouse at the far end, crossed the river where we reached it. In very high water we'd come to look, not fish, for tangles of logs would tumble over and fill up a backwater almost at our feet. In that backwater, when the river was still high but clear enough to fish, people now and again caught flathead catfish weighing forty or fifty pounds. I actually saw one or two of them.

We'd speculate on trying that ourselves, but it was not, after all, our kind of fishing. (If my father had been a different man, this would be a different story.) On a summer morning when the river was peaceful, we'd walk down around the dam with our rods—my father's rod and my jointed cane pole, at first—and minnow bucket and tackle bag, and make our way downstream over tumbled stone. Out in the middle was what we called a sandbar, more like an island with cottonwoods running down its spine. A concrete wall, a popular place to sit and fish, connected the sandbar with the lip of the dam.

When the water was low, or anyway not too high, you could wade out to the bar and fish for catfish anywhere around it. Now this in particular is what I remember:

That sandbar, the first time we fished the Blue, was the Promised Land. Maybe we'd met somebody who told us that was where the fish were, maybe we even saw a fisherman—a native—carrying a big stringer of catfish back across; anyway that was where I, at seven or eight, had to go or die. Only I couldn't go; my father, fuss and fume as I might, wouldn't. Not safe, in his opinion, the only one that counted. He was a cautious man, his take on it proves nothing in itself, but maybe it really wasn't. Wading knee-deep or deeper in the current, in tennis shoes on slick invisible rocks? Gear in one hand, me—small for my age, a non-swimmer, tangled up with his leg as I lurched and fought for footing—in the other?

Still: what was the risk of drowning compared to *getting there*? Wouldn't the river, anyway, have parted for a couple of guys named Moses?

It really was the Promised Land. Later that summer or the next, the water maybe lower, we did cross. I don't know if this was the first time, but it's the one that matters: I'm sitting on the wall with my feet dangling over the water, the concrete rough against my bare skin. I'm holding in my hands a cane pole, an unwieldy object maybe not suitable for vaulting, but it felt like it—nine or ten feet long, with a pole's length of stout fish line tied on; tied onto that a hook baited with a dead minnow, dead because of being threaded onto the hook, with a sinker clipped on above to carry the bait to the bottom. You don't cast with a rig like that; with the pole at a forty-five-degree angle to the water, you release the sinker and let nature take its course. Nevertheless: first cast. Because sometime thereafter—a few minutes, half an hour, no time at all—the line straightens out. The tip of the pole dips, and I'm sitting there with no clear awareness that what is happening is what's *supposed* to happen. My father, sitting next to me, knows. "Pull!" Now landing a small fish with a cane pole is simple enough—you haul it straight up out of the water, and when it whacks you in the face, you've landed it. Only this, I need no experience to tell me, is not a small fish. I pull sideways—to the right, being left-handed, like a left-handed batter—and fortunately in that direction there's a gravel shelf at the foot of the wall, onto which I drag the fish. It's a big one. The Big One. Bigger than the nine-pound flathead catfish I caught out of the Blue, years later; than the sixteen-pound pike from the Lake of the Woods in Canada; than the forty-three-inch muskie from this very Susquehanna where, after quite a long pause, my son Jeremy has twitched his lure for the second time.

To be literal about it, it was a channel catfish seventeen inches long. One pound twelve ounces precisely, on my mother's kitchen scale. *That's* all? Only consider this: challenged to remember anything else that happened that year, maybe the year before or after, I'd come up empty. We went fishing, of course. Mild summer water rose around my knees, river-sand filled my sneakers, but my next big fish? Nocturnal swimmer in the River of Time. That seventeen-inch monolith rises out of a blank ocean.

I do remember small fish—what's a fishing childhood, inland and far from any trout stream, without bluegills? Mostly they were pumpkinseeds, in fact, a more colorful related sunfish; unimpressed by their orange-and-blue iridescence, we took them home and ate them. Pottawatamie, like all lakes in Kansas, was an artificial impoundment maybe dating back to the Civilian Conservation Corps days of the Great Depression. A few acres only, hardly more than a big pond. At first a woman who lived in an old house nearby sold bait and rented boats. Then she departed and the house burned to a skeleton, and we fished from shore until years later when, home from the Army, I bought the Grumman canoe. Sometimes my mother came along and all three of us fished; she was there on the day of my fall from grace:

Picture, then, this little family perched on the earth-and-stone dam that formed the lake, all three of us with worms under bobbers— fishing Norman-Rockwell-style. My parents are using droopy old bamboo fly rods, I've got my cane pole with which, because it's longer, I can reach farther out into the water. *Which just happens to be where the biggest fish are.* Therefore, at the age of eight I am *outfishing my parents*. My father comments on this, possibly with veiled envy. I swell up twice my size. Fishing is good. Catching fish is better. Catching more fish and bigger fish than anyone around you is best of all. (How many steps, from here, to $50,000 bass tournaments and your very own fishing show?)

And then, suddenly, you grow up—to about twelve, at which point what you want to do is get away from the old man and catch something all by yourself. Which might have been a bit of a trick, four years shy of my first driving license, if not for Wildcat Creek. Up a hill from our house, trek the edge of Sunset Cemetery from front to back, scramble down a long cedar-tangled slope, there it was—a chocolate-colored tributary of the Kaw River, a place to get muddy and fish-slimed and happy all over.

I knew it first from minnow-seining expeditions for the river trips—no bait shops around Manhattan in those days or none we cared to frequent. (Few know it now, but bait you dig or catch yourself *satisfies*—the fisherman, if not the fish.) We'd scramble down with our bucket and seine, a flat fine-meshed net maybe four-by-six-feet tied to sticks on either side, with weights at the bottom and floats at the top. Holding it at an obtuse angle to the surface, one to each stick, all we had to do then was walk it upstream through shallow riffles; three or four passes caught more little fish than we needed. Back home, the bucket sat in the basement sink overnight with water dribbling into it, ready for the next morning's early start. We fished the creek together too sometimes, drifting bait in the riffles for small catfish, and set out trotlines overnight; those came up slack and empty until, one day, "Pull!" my father said. I pulled, and brought up half of a channel catfish, the rest eaten away by crayfish or turtles. In life it would have weighed two or three pounds, by far the biggest catfish we ever saw in that creek.

All that was good. Going alone—once I'd learned to swim, my mother's non-negotiable price of admission—was better. Listen, there are things you need to do on which the most sympathetic father is a dead drag—a half-eaten catfish tied to your ankle. Such as shooting bullfrogs between the eyes with a B-B gun. At least once I brought them home and skinned out the legs, which, my mother having been press-ganged into service, leapt in the frying pan. Or sinking chunks of liver into the murk to coax out crayfish—some of whose ultimate fate illustrates the hazard of failing to let go. Or just hanging out with my mutt Ginger, a bizarrely bearded terrier-and-who-knows-what who swam about placid and buoyant as a duck; one day she got a water snake between her jaws and, with a rat-terrier's flip of the head, flung it three feet into the air. I hope it is clear that all this was, despite the absence of fish, fishing. In spirit. Yet I would not have forgotten my rod.

The common carp is a humble fish, underrated in this country. In parts of Europe they're an entertainment industry; my British neighbor told me of carp lakes to which access is severely limited, requiring reservations weeks or months in advance. (To which I could only reply, silently, God bless America.) In parts of Asia, a reliable protein source. In Kansas in the fifties, in any state you could name to this day, a fisher-child's dream come true. They can live in any sort of stagnant soup—if ever we succeed in destroying the life of this planet, there will remain, nonetheless, cockroaches in the air, brown rats on the land, carp in the water. They're plentiful. Being vegetarians, always amply fed, they get big—in most waters up to twenty pounds or more. They fight like hell. A trout fishing acquaintance who'd been out West told me the trout guides referred to them as Idaho bonefish—bonefish being legendary fighters of saltwater flats. Best of all, to the North American palate they're inedible, sharply reducing competition from grownups. Beyond all that, in the concoction of baits—exotically flavored doughballs, mostly—they're a challenge to ingenuity. Some theorize that carp are powerfully attracted to strawberry gelatin. Or vanilla. Or . . . how many famous chefs got their start with doughballs?

One day, fishing alone in a turgid pool in Wildcat Creek, I caught a six-pound carp. Now that, in Kansas, is one hell of a big fish. Bigger than all but the most freakish of bass, than all but a very few catfish. Naturally I brought it home—how, otherwise, would I have known it weighed six pounds? Naturally—what else were we going to do with it? Get it mounted?—my mother was called upon to cook it for dinner. Now I hold no fixed opinion about a dish, a theoretical dish, which might be entitled Carp of Paradise. To prepare, place a carp in a limpid pool for at least one year, feeding it on sweet corn and blueberries. Filet, press out the noxious juices, marinate in a delicately flavored broth. Cut into fingers, bread with cornmeal laced generously with Cajun spices, fry quickly. Serve with hearty side dishes, just in case. Only my mother, hampered by the meat-and-potatoes tastes of the men in her life, was a plain-and-simple cook. I'm not sure if she baked or fried it; what I do know is that, while carp makes wholesome dog food, a dog who eats too much of it smells.

To my father—born in Minnesota, raised there and in Wisconsin during his early years—the Blue River was never truly home. He yearned for the north country, and so, starting with the August when I was ten, to the lower edge of it we went—to a housekeeping resort called Pine Terrace (practically everything up that way seems to be Pine Something), just six cabins on a chain of lakes in central Minnesota. I'd never been taken anywhere in my life except to Tennessee to visit my mother's relatives, which was all right, but woefully fishless. Now, for weeks, we'd been going over the tackle. I'd never fished with anything but bait, but in Minnesota, the name itself evocative as a temple bell, we were going to use artificials. Not soulless wood and metal contraptions (never, at least, plastic in those days) new from the store, but lures with pedigrees. Dardevles and Red Eyes—convex metal baits which wobbled and flashed in the water, aptly termed spoons; Pikie Minnows, plugs the size, shape, almost the color of cigars, with which my father and his father before him had caught big fish in Canada, long before I was born. We shined up the spoons with silver polish, sharpened the big treble hooks. I held them in my hands and their power made my hair stand up.

We loaded up the trunk of the '41 Plymouth, which, at forty-five miles an hour, would take us north. The alarm went off at three o'clock the next morning, by 3:30 we were on our way with lightning flickering on the southern horizon behind us. Nebraska by daylight, Minnesota by late afternoon. Then actual lakes. By noon the next day, at the end of a mile-long sandy road winding through scrub pines, the first glimpse of green Star Lake, our August home for the next eight or nine years.

Six small, brown cabins spread out along the shore, at the left end of the row the owners' brown house, not much bigger—mere details. Detail: for our cabin my father was paying the astonishing sum—this was 1954—of forty-five dollars a week, with the boat thrown in. A massive wooden rowboat, sixteen feet long, moored to a dock on which I could stand, look down into the water, and see . . . actual fish! Hand-sized bluegills, true—my hand's size—but still, fish, thirty feet from our front (only) door. Across and to the left was a bay, actually the narrow end of the lake, with lily pads clustered at its edges. Invisible in the undergrowth was the outlet of a creek flowing out of another, smaller lake, Beaver, accessible by way of a half-mile portage. The resort maintained a single boat on it, to which, the first year or two before they finally instituted a signup system, you staked your claim by getting up earlier than anyone else. (And nobody got up earlier than the Moses men.) The grassy track at dawn would be dew-soaked; little spiders, hundreds of them, caught dew in their webs each night. When you got to a certain dip in the path, the air grew colder. The boat's seats would be chilled and slick. The mist shrouding the lake not clearly air, the lake itself not clearly water. To the right, Star Lake wound away out of sight for a mile or so, its shoreline all natural except for the stretch on which we stood, wooded, birch and pine and alder. On the last day of every trip, my father would toss the birch leaf he'd carried in his wallet for the past year into the lake, and replace it with a new one.

That first day, within an hour, I was seated in the stern of that ponderous boat, rod in my trembling hand, as my father propelled us out onto the lake. By pulling on oars, seven or seven-and-a-half feet long. No motor. Everyone else used motors, five-horse Evinrudes that the resort rented, but we, with fine scorn for the noisy effete multitudes, rowed. Across to the far shore, probably out of some sense that fish would hang out as far from human habitation as possible, where I did not fling out the first cast of my new fishing life. The rod was a steel baitcasting rod, the reel had a free-spinning spool, and you cast by applying just enough pressure with the ball of your thumb to shoot the line out under control. Otherwise it would backlash, and you'd spend the next one to ten minutes picking at the resulting bird's nest, swiftly going crazy. So I trolled, dragged a Red Eye spoon behind the boat as my father contoured the shore. The first thing that happened was that I got stung on the cheek by a wasp. The second was that something whacked my lure. I reeled in with the rod bending until I could see down in the water a long shadow, my father scooped with the landing net, and I had caught a northern pike. Which did not greatly resemble an ordinary bass-shaped fish. No one could ever have convinced me that it was in fact a small northern pike, little more than what's called a snake or a hammer handle. It might have weighed a pound. It was a foot-and-a-half long, mottled green and slimy with a mouthful of needle-sharp teeth, native to nowhere-near-Kansas. To Minnesota. And any specimen of a species of fish which grows to over forty pounds carries within and about it pure trembling potential. On the last day of that trip I caught a four-and-a-half-pounder, better than two feet long. Somebody lost one on Beaver Lake which, he said, would have gone four feet. Had it right up to the boat. Measured it by eye against the oar. I was hooked. I was home.

In the lakes of that chain you could catch little bluegills off the dock, classic kid-fishing, or off that same dock get outlandishly lucky and land a seven-pound pike. In Beaver Lake at night, bullheads by dangling hooks baited with bacon over the weed beds. Nice crappies in the evening by casting little white jigs into dark water, tree-reflecting; you'd know to strike when the jig disappeared. One day we dragged our boat up the marshy alder-tangled creek which fed Beaver Lake to yet another, smaller lake, Sunset; dragged it over a beaver dam, in the pool above which we caught bluegills as fast as we could drop in a hook. *Lunker* bluegills—in memory.

In later years, as recorded in my father's journal, the fishing got pretty slow:

> 9 Aug., Thursday [1962]: Though the morning was cold and cloudy, with an east wind, fish bit fairly well (though short-striking somewhat) before breakfast: 2 bass and a pike landed, and others missed (Big Star). The forenoon, like other forenoons of late, looked good but produced almost nothing: 1 small pike. Beaver about noon the same. Elizabeth found many mushrooms. Raspberries. To Beaver in the evening, but only 2 pike and 1 tiny bass; evening fishing except for the first 2 evenings has been worthless. One of the pike about 2-3/4 (Elizabeth). Saw an osprey, the first I recall seeing here, fly over toward Sunset with a good-sized fish. Beautiful still moonlight night, quite cool. (George says it went to 39 degrees last night.) Much beaver activity.

But what does this signify next to this memory from our first year: the last morning at the resort, and for once, what with packing up, we've missed out on the Beaver Lake boat. Only for this one year there's a second boat there, a half-derelict owned by a man who had died. What became of it thereafter is lost; I do know that for me, no image is more powerful than that of a wooden rowboat sunk in shallow water, with lilies growing through its planks. This boat, anyway, floats us out onto the lake, into which I drop a leopard frog that I myself had caught the day before. A dozen or a hundred slow oar strokes later, my bait stops dead. With bated breath I slack off the line, which now takes on a life of its own, slides down and away into that element into which we cannot see far, and . . . *Now.* I haul back on the rod, which bends irresistibly to the surface, and after a mighty struggle bring up a three-pound bass. Nothing much to a southern or even midwestern adult angler—but this is Minnesota and I am ten years old. This fish is half again as big as any other we've seen during the whole two weeks. It is the biggest fish I ever caught, or hope to. In memory.

At fishing resorts, the story is always that they were biting like crazy last week—and are sure to be the week after you leave. Here, the mythical month was June. We could never come in June, because my father had or felt that he had to teach summer school. Some years later, after we'd moved on to bigger, more northerly waters, I stopped by in June on my way home from college. The owner took me on a circuit of Beaver Lake, an hour or more of hard casting; I never saw or felt a fish. Sometime after that he mentioned in a Christmas card that "There's some changes going on around here." That casual sentence triggered years of nightmares, real night horrors. Lakes built up with houses, amusement parks, I'd wake up thrashing and sweating. It was a back corner of Minnesota, not coastal Florida, and probably what he was talking about was a few cottages. But I have no plans to go and find out.

Last Christmas I went to visit my parents, now in their mid-eighties, after some years away. One afternoon, while they napped, I walked up the hill, along the edge of the cemetery, and down the long tangled slope to Wildcat Creek. The creek bottom and the stream itself were unchanged, uncannily so after forty years; I could identify riffles where I'd fished for catfish, pools into which I'd cast doughballs for carp. The water on this mild winter day ran green in bright sunlight. I took away with me a clamshell, iridescent pink inside and nearly the size of my hand. Another day I drove alone to the Blue River, which, the place we fished, was changed. Access was from the far side, to a formally designated "Rocky Ford Fishing Area," and in places the channel had been sculpted to improve habitat. There were walleye and bass in the water now, winter-green water, but a fisherman I asked said the fishing was poor. Looked better than it was, he said. I had not, by design, borrowed one of my father's rods. The sandbar looked as it always had. As I walked down the bank beside it, I came upon the skull of a gar, a primitive armored fish with elongated needle-toothed jaws that must, in life, have been close to three feet long. This I carried back to Pennsylvania, faintly surprised that it failed to set off the airport security alarms, and placed on my writing desk.

Now, home again, I'm attuned to nightmare. Story about a flood-control dike? But it turns out to be a limited project, shoring up a low-lying creek bank a mile or more from the river. Riverfront park planned? But that's upstream and it's good news—more people with more of a stake in water quality. The North Central Pennsylvania Conservancy is working on a river conservation plan. All clear so far. Jeremy retrieves his first cast of the morning, finally, throws out another and another as I work us out into midstream. Below, to the left of the landing as we face the far shore, the West Branch breaks off in riffles to both sides of a large island—half a mile long, maybe, densely timbered, the first of three on our route. To the left the riffle runs shallow; in low water you can easily ford it, and we might have to get out and drag the canoe. Below that, a pool which in a hundred yards or so shelves up and becomes a flat; then an islet, more riffles, a timber-studded pool below; another flat, another riffle down near the bottom of the large island. Gorgeous water the whole way down—and nearly empty of fish. We might, on a good day, raise one or two, hardly enough to retard our sense of outrage. There ought to be fish here—why aren't there?

The ways of fish are not only stranger than we know; they are, as someone said of the quantum, stranger than we *can* know. Chaos theory explains why: minute differences in initial conditions, immeasurable in the aggregate, produce wildly unpredictable outcomes. That's why the slightest changes in conditions at the time this planet was formed would have meant, almost certainly, no fish and no us. It's why no one will ever be able to predict the weather more than a few days in advance. (Considering the number of thunderstorms we've been caught in, even a few hours is sometimes iffy.) Now add to that the fact that experience is not transferable. As Deepak Chopra put it in *How to Know God*, "If my dog or cat was staring right at God, it would do me no good because I don't share their nervous systems." Still less do we share the piscine nervous system. Dissect smallmouth bass till you're waist-deep in guts, observe them daily for ten lifetimes, and all you'll collect is tendencies. But what will *this* particular fish do when presented with *that* lure under *these* conditions? Nobody knows. And *what* conditions, anyway? The river is not, by its nature it can never be, the same from moment to moment. Stand in the living water: that water passes on by. Newtonian cause and effect, the notion that with enough data and enough formulas we could chart the course of every physical object in the universe from now to the end of time, is out the window. We can no more call the fish in this river to our lures than, with ritual however hallowed, call God.

To the right of the island, down the far side of the river, there's fifty yards of heavy water—foot-high standing waves—and then the rock-bottomed channel, today no more than two or three feet deep, settles into a steady and easy flow. Here we sometimes do well. "Which way?" I ask—a weighty question, for the choice, once made, is irrevocable. Once into the riffle on either side, down we go; skunked on the right, we can wonder till crows fly backwards if today was the day for the left. Down we go, all the way to Muncy, whatever the mood of the fish or the fishermen, or the sky. Thirty percent chance of afternoon thunderstorms, the Weather Service reports; but if you let a forecast like that deter you, you hardly get out at all.

"Right," Jeremy replies. There are sightseers—tourists—and then there are fishermen. For a fisherman it's no choice at all.

Getting down to the right requires some tricky navigation. Across from the landing lies yet another islet behind which flows a narrow shadowed stream with the feel of a bayou. In today's low water, after negotiating a flat that adds a scratch and a scrape or two to our hard-worked boat, we keep that islet tight to starboard. We duck under a downed tree, rods stowed inboard, and then, kneeling to keep the center of gravity low, turn hard left into the channel. Out with a friend one day last summer in our other craft, a twelve-foot johnboat, we didn't quite make that turn. Or I, the oarsman, didn't. In the middle of the channel was a half-submerged flat rock, angled with the high edge downstream, which we hit side-on. The upstream gunwale went under, all loose gear went downstream; we scrambled out and down the rocky bank and got everything back, so that was fine, except that the boat itself was wedged onto the rock by several hundred pounds of fast-flowing water. Looking and feeling more and more, as we pushed and pulled, tugged and hauled, like a natural feature of the stream; it would float on down when the river rose (but there was no rain in the forecast that day) and lifted it off.

Now it seems evident, since that boat now lies bottom-up in a corner of our back yard, that in time we did shift it. So, apparently, did my father's father shift the flat-bottomed wooden boat that he rowed hard onto a flat stump in the Wisconsin River, seventy-five or eighty years ago. Here is the last verse of the poem my father wrote about it:

> The struggle in darkness, shoving, shifting;
> The empty heaving at a useless fulcrum—
> I remember these. Growing silent
> And listening, so, to the smallest sounds of darkness,
> The plops and gurgles near, and the tiny
> Rustling and calling in the dark shoreward—
> I remember that. What I do not remember
> Is ever feeling pine wood moving on pine wood
> Until we were off. Can I say that we did get off?
> Or do we sit in a boat on a carrying river
> That bears and brings us the life we live
> In boynight, near Wausau, Wisconsin?

Today we make the turn neatly, well short of the rock, bounce over the standing waves, and now, with the island between us and the landing, the only visible work of human hands is the railway line carved into the high bank. We pass a great blue heron—motionless, all functional curves—waiting on its rock for a minnow or crayfish to happen within range of its long, snaky neck. Further down a family of mergansers, fifteen half-grown, fish-eating ducks with their mother, swim along the edge of the river ahead of us. We slide on down, both of us casting now, into the flow of the day.

three
_____

Catch and Release

In the low water I keep the canoe well out in the channel, so we'll have room to cast both ways. Soaking a bait on the bottom, as in my childhood Blue River catfishing, you can daydream. As much as to catch something, in fact, *stillness* is what still-fishing's about. This is more like playing center field in a baseball game—not some Charlie Brown kids' game where your first intimation of action is the ball whacking you on the head, but the real thing (minus, thank God, the fans). As every pitch is delivered you're crouched on the balls of your feet, looking for that split-second jump that could translate to a half step, three extra feet at the end of your sprint, an out instead of a triple. And this despite your knowledge that the odds are fifty to one, maybe, against your having to do anything at all. Then between pitches, while the pitcher is scuffing up the ball, getting himself together, your work is to relax. Shake every muscle loose. Deep, slow breaths. Now: ready. Here we go again. So it is with this surface bass fishing. The prop baits we're using have to be fished with a twitch-pause, twitch-pause to imitate a helplessly crippled baitfish, which means that during the pauses there's a little slack in the line. Once in a great while you might see a ripple behind the lure, an intimation of life; ordinarily, though, there's no warning at all. A whacking splash like the crack of the bat, then in a heartbeat, unless you're wide awake, poised to strike back like that center fielder who had better be moving *before* the sound reaches him, nothing. All as it was except for the pounding of your heart, and that flat feeling that goes with a chance irrevocably lost. Sounded like a big one, too. Damn. *Why wasn't I paying attention?*

A fine reason to be out here on the river in the early mist: there's not a soul in sight. No liquored-up loonies to throw beer bottles at you for missing a strike. Another: you're pitcher and center fielder in one, the pace of the day your own. Hypothetically. If you're not too hungry-needy. If what you're looking for above all is action, each new cast can hit the water within five seconds of the last one's coming out. Otherwise, slow down a little. Scan the shores and the sky for birds. Be where you are.

It's early, and we're looking for action. A sign from the river, vindicating hope; we've fished in waters which have taught us, viscerally, what hopelessness is all about. I'm throwing my left-handed casts leftwards, out toward the island; keeping them short, because the fish mostly hit during the first few feet of retrieve. And I'm focused (it's early), so hear rather than see the splash from the right side. My head jerks around and I see what I hope to, Jeremy's rod bending. A moment later, forty feet toward shore and a little downstream, the fish jumps all the way out, a clear two feet into the air, and shakes. One time out of three on these first jumps, even if you're quick and keep the line tight, the lure goes flying. Three or four years ago, before Jeremy had caught enough fish to take them as they come and go, those jumps occasioned many a silent prayer: *Oh please. Oh please. Thank you, God.* (And hang on; it's far from over yet.) Even now you could hardly say we're calm—if you're going to remain calm on a rollercoaster, why ride?—though the fish is not large. It's a nice one, though—nice keeper. What we are is happy and busy. I'm maneuvering the canoe, trying to keep the fish out from under. Jeremy's keeping the rod tip high and pretty much hanging on as the line slices the surface in wild rapid arcs and zigzags; then he's able to recover line, yard by yard, until the fish is swimming around within six feet of the boat.

I put down the paddle and pick up the landing net. Overplaying a fish is not good for its health, and I would like to land it quickly and gracefully. I have never forgotten my father's butchering the netting of a pike bigger than any I'd yet caught, early in that first Pine Terrace trip. He tried to fold it into the net crosswise instead of taking it headfirst, and it flopped off the hook and free into the water—lucky fish. I was six years younger then than Jeremy is today. This is not a fish of the sort that can yank a prayer out of you at any age. But still. Only Jeremy is sitting eight feet away from me in the bow, so that, though we're leaning toward each other as best we might, mindful of swamping (this boat is hardly what they call a stable fishing platform), I'm far from the center of the fish's arc. And it's not completely played out. And the light's not all that great. The result is a couple of missed swipes and a sense of muddling about; finally, though, I do get the fish in the net and lift it aboard.

It's beautiful, a dark, wild West Branch smallmouth maybe

fourteen inches long.

It mustn't remain long out of the water. I hand the net to Jeremy, pick up the paddle and begin working us back upstream; we've drifted down fifty yards or more, good water we don't want to miss. Jeremy, having set down his rod and wet his hands, grips the fish by the lower jaw and twitches the hook out—one hook luckily out of the six on the two trebles. It comes out easily because we've pinched the barb down, for that very reason—at a potential cost, we thought when we started doing that, of losing fish, but in fact we've done at least as well as ever. Yet one more fishing myth exposed: barbed hooks get a superior grip on anchor ropes and ear lobes, truly, not on fish. Jeremy now displays the fish in both hands, for two seconds maybe, before lowering it over the side into the water. It darts away out of sight in an instant—one hell of a confused fish, one given to anthropomorphizing might say. But then if you do that, and work through the implications, you can't help but give up fishing. Alive and well, let's rather say, handled with tender loving care.

No talk, all this time. Now:

"All right, Jer. Nice catch."

"Thanks."

Which is all that's required, though what I might add—but don't, for it's long gone without saying—is, "Nice release."

My son is a weird kid of the finest kind. Anyone who's hung out around fishing resort docks knows the formula: the smaller the children, the smaller the dead fish. (Whether dragged in off the water on stringers or left floating in buckets at the end of the day.) Most people, most male people—do little girls also have the urge but have it socialized out of them?—at a certain age need to kill things. Some go on to become deer hunters, thereby at least providing, as any Pennsylvania farmer would tell you, a useful environmental service; some become killers on Wall Street; some become animal rights activists of the most violent and frightening kind. Jeremy, ever since he caught his first legal bass and so faced his first life-or-death choice, has been blooming into a balanced ethicist. Killing simply to kill—coyotes, bobcats, recently an eagle—is a misbegotten relic of the Old Stone Age. Deer hunters, given that the coyotes are too few to limit the population and that a deer, at least, translates into venison, he puts up with. On recent trips off the Jersey coast, when Keith and I have filled a cooler with flounder and weakfish, he's put up with us. What he says nevertheless, of people who keep fish, is "I don't see how they can square it with their conscience." This is by no means a simple issue. A non-fishing acquaintance, a devout man, says of catch-and-release fishing that he couldn't bring himself to put them through that. The fish, that is, through the panicky struggle, though even *panicky* begs some questions about the piscine nervous system. Our acquaintance puts up with us graciously; Jeremy defends us on grounds of ultimate harmlessness, I because I must live with myself and, at this time in my life, fish. As well defend a cocaine habit, on grounds of ravishing delight? So be it. Still: though a 12-inch bass, transmuted in an hour from riverine quicksilver to filets fried golden, surely rivals cocaine; though the removal of half a dozen out of the hundred or more we catch in a summer would do little to the fishery; though I do still get hungry sometimes, none of that, with my son's eyes on me, quite suffices. I no longer keep bass out of the West Branch.

If you're hungry enough, conscience is a ladder leaning against a different tree. One law for hospitality to strangers, another for filling your belly. Only there's hunger and hunger. How many people in this country, I wonder, fish with hook and line out of real physical need? If the perch aren't biting, their kids might go protein-hungry, I mean, and their fishing is cost-effective. Add up outlay for tackle, depreciation, and transportation, how much a pound are they paying? If less than market price, there's nothing to say but good luck. *You,* however, you in the ten-thousand-dollar bass boat—what's your excuse?

"Have you ever tasted fresh-caught walleye? Fried up over an open fire after a long morning on the water?" (The bass-boater might inquire.)

"As a matter of fact I have."

"So who needs an excuse?"

For aesthetic hunger, that is. You live far from an ocean or a Great Lake, you crave the real thing? Better catch it yourself. A viewpoint with which I couldn't agree more, intellectually, but with which I have, viscerally, some idiosyncratic difficulties. All because my father, back in those Pine Terrace days, was a hungry man.

I've never heard, I can hardly conceive, of a fish hunger like it. The catfish and bluegills we caught back home in Kansas couldn't begin to keep up with it. So at Pine Terrace, for two, three, four weeks every summer, we ate fish twice a day. Nothing wrong with that in itself, we're not talking about hard drugs or liquor here, if it calls you. If that hunger is more than physical, even, if those bass and crappie, perch and bluegill fill some long-forgotten childhood emptiness. The problematical word, however, is *we.* Now here I must put suspicion to rest: my father was no tyrant. He was a poet, with a poet's imagination, but poetry was poetry and fish was fish, and the notion that we, *family,* might care less for fish than he did was simply beyond him. It was one of those truths too dark to speak: fish twice a day was making me gag. Literally. Forty-five years later, my throat tightens at the thought of it. Again I feel my sheer sensuous relief at the sight, the all-too-rare sight, of bacon and eggs for breakfast.

I gag on one bite too many of fish to this very day—fresh fried fish, that is, the real thing. To those who keep fish simply because they taste so damn good, therefore, I have only this to say: first, *don't* drag them around on a stringer all day. Not only is this an inhumane practice, it half-spoils your treat. Rather, whack them on the head at once, bleed them by slicing the gill rakers, and place them on a bed of ice. And second, enjoy. In loving tribute to my father.

But then, you there on the dock, you're not holding up that stringer of walleye just because they're tasty—are you? Really, what's the use of a limit of walleye hidden away in an ice chest? We—collectively as a gender—carry our dead bucks on the roof rack, disingenuously protesting that there's no room in the trunk. Scalp our fallen enemies and wear their hair on our belts. Notch our six-guns, paint pictures of downed bombers on our fighter planes. Collect trophies for Little League baseball, Peewee football, soccer, wrestling, bowling. Deer heads (expensive) or racks (cheap). Dead fish. One day, coming off the river down at Muncy, we met a guy with a bass. It was twenty inches long, he told us, and he was getting it mounted. It was sixteen, seventeen at the outside; with some difficulty I restrained myself from offering him my tape measure. (I wonder if it kept on seeming big enough to him, considered as a wall hanging, or if finally, too long dead to eat, it ended up buried.) Also we call the newspaper. One day the local paper ran a picture of a couple of guys with half a dozen beautiful trout, eighteen to twenty inches or more. A few days later, a follow-up story: they'd been arrested for stealing breeders from a state hatchery.

Deep down we're Beowulf, howling our challenge to the indifferent sky. Nowadays Beowulf has a website: mydickisbiggerthanyou rdick.com.

As a fisherman in this age of limits, though, Beowulf has some problems. Legal limits: no more than six bass at least twelve inches long, and your current resident—*non*-resident, thank you, for invaders from Denmark—Pennsylvania Angler's Permit must be displayed prominently on your person at all times. With trout stamp if so inclined, catch and release bass fishing only until the second Saturday in June, boat must be registered, Personal Flotation Devices on board (try and swim deep enough to get at Grendel's Dam wearing a PFD), Special Regulations apply, thank you very much.

And ecological limits: the carrying capacity of a Canadian lake divided by fisherman-hours as governed by the driving time from Toronto. Or of a Pennsylvania river—did I say six bass twelve inches or more? Sorry, I meant *four* bass *fifteen* inches or more. And what one might call contextual limits: suppose that bass at the Muncy landing really had been twenty inches long, and the guy did get it mounted, and it impressed the hell out of his buddies the first time they saw it. What's he going to do with the *next* twenty-inch bass he catches? Because from the moment he kills it, or it just dies from being dragged around the river, the clock is ticking. That is the salient fact about dead fish. If you don't do something about them pretty damn quick, they stink.

Whoever said that fish and houseguests stink after *three* days was not a fisherman.

So here we are in the kitchen, around ten o'clock at night, with fifty dead bluegill. Real nice ones, let's say, eight-to-ten inches long.

This particular scenario is inspired by the misadventures of Bobby Knight, the legendary basketball coach. When too many tantrums combined with too few wins finally lost him his job at Indiana, he said most poignantly, about having to move, that in Indiana he could catch fifty bluegill in an hour. It's difficult to envision Bobby Knight as a catch-and-release fisherman, and with bluegill, anyway, who does? That's why they're known as panfish. Leaving the coach to cope with his as best he can, then, here we are with ours. In a wire basket in the sink, let's say, one or two maybe flopping a little, but we'll assume that's reflex. Dishpan half full of water for the leavings. Counter thickly spread with newspaper. Now:

We could scale and filet; filet and skin; or scale and just hack off the heads, scoop out the guts, call it a night. At Pine Terrace in the fish cleaning house, a screen-fronted shed with a long counter and big sinks, bare light bulbs dangling from the rafters, we scaled and hacked. You can dress out a bluegill that way in a minute or two, leaving the bones in for the consumer to cope with—white ribs the size of straight pins, camouflaged in the flaky white flesh. In memory I stare unhappily, tight-throated, at a plate containing more than one such fish. "A nice mess of fish" was what we brought in, or on a particularly bounteous day, "That'll be good for a couple of messes." I was eleven or twelve years old, out in the fresh air all day long, hungry. Only for something else. So maybe, after all, we'll filet these fifty. It takes longer; lacking a sharp, flexible knife and a sure hand it's wasteful; and with small fish like these, at night when you're tired, you'll quite likely slice off a bit of your finger. Not on your dominant hand, though, and it will grow back, and you'll end up with thin little filets which, breaded and fried up crisp, will crunch right down. With not many bones at all—a few rib ends, as my father used to put it when anyone complained— which you can swallow without even noticing.

First, though, these fifty fish have to be scaled. Fileting and skinning would be quicker, but we're going to scale because that's how we've always done it. And because the skin of a small fried fish is good, the way chicken skin is good, and damn the cholesterol. Also because this provides the boy in the case—m e—with a job to do not involving deadly edge tools. Imagine an implement like a wide-bladed table knife, only saw-toothed on both sides and the blunt end. Bend the teeth up at right angles. You've got a scaler. Now hold the fish as steady as possible with the head toward you, and go to work from tail to head as if raking leaves. Don't forget the belly; cover the entire edible surface with care, for it's shameful if the fileter must, without comment, clean up unscaled patches with his knife. Likewise if he has to wait for you, so, as a wise country artist so aptly put it, keep a-goin'. Thirty seconds into this operation, which is taking place under cold kitchen lights, somewhere between an hour and three days past bedtime, scales are on the floor, walls, ceiling, your shirt, your hair, and the dog, who, being a long-haired dog, will be shedding scales for the next week and a half. Which is about how much time seems to pass before you're done. Three fish ahead of your partner. Glory be. Now all that remains is to rinse lightly the one hundred filets, place them in half a dozen plastic freezer boxes, and—a ttention, fish lovers—c over them with cold water because fish, to stay fresh, must be frozen wet. Now to the freezer. *Not* tripping on the steps, *not* dumping those boxes into the bowels of the basement—t hat would be good. Half a dozen nice messes! What a day! Are we done?

Well, not quite. What remains is that dishpan containing the fifty carcasses, and you can't have thought—can you?—we were just going to dump them in the garbage. With collection not due till next Thursday? No, they have now got to be buried. In the dead of night, like something the police might come looking for sometime, by flashlight, along with the top few scaly-slimy layers of newspaper. Hold that light steady on the hole. Do it right. Don't forget about the dog.

Get your shower, now. Fish slime in its essence being impervious to anything less than a wire brush and lye, make it a good one. Go to bed with the south wind stirring the curtains, your fingers stinging and cramped. What you'll see on the screen behind your eyes is not the rod bending, fish circling to the surface, splash and sparkle, but blood and bone and scale.

Was it truly necessary to keep that many fish?

One day in my later teens, in a Kansas backwater, I caught, and kept, *fifty small carp*. For dog food. The memory of the newspaper headline that must have inspired such folly, "Critical Dog Food Shortage Looms," somehow eludes me.

On the second morning of our first trip to the Jersey Shore, Keith and I got into the weakfish—beautiful silvery sea trout. We went ashore for lunch, leaving our rented boat at the rim of a gently shelving beach. The photo on my refrigerator shows me in tee-shirt and swim trunks, left hand raised with thumb up, twenty-two fish rowed up on the sand at my feet. Be a good idea to get those fish dressed out, we thought. Save trouble later. While we dressed them, the tide ran out. There sat our boat, high and dry. There sat the two of us for the next three hours.

There's such a thing, even, as catching too many fish, too easily. Try telling that to the men who extinguished the passenger pigeon.

They fired at random into the sky, no more able to miss than, standing under an old maple in high summer, miss leaves. To the men who decimated the bison. The men who clamor to hunt the elk, domestic animals with antlers, which have been planted in Pennsylvania. Yet one day last spring I drove an hour to the main stem of the Susquehanna River, a place where a dam is inflated—great sausages of what looks like heavy canvas—each summer to make a pool for boaters upstream. It wasn't inflated yet; off one end of it and slightly downstream was a backwater, then a shallow gravel bar, then, flowing fast from left to right as I faced it, the wide river. I stood knee-deep on the bar in my waders and cast a yellow jig—quarter-ounce lead head mounted on the shank of a hook with a flexible plastic tail threaded on, a fifteen-cent lure—into the edge of the current. For three hours I averaged a strike every three or four casts, all from smallmouth bass in the twelve-to-fifteen-inch range. In those three hours I caught thirty-two fish, close to a third of what we land in a normal summer's fishing. I could have stayed on, brought it up to forty, fifty, but I was bored. Life, real life, is not like that.

Memo to Coach Knight: How many times each summer do you *want* to catch fifty bluegill in an hour?

But then, I suppose, it is not possible to win too many basketball games.

In real life, this morning on this river, my lure is the center of a whacking splash. I yank right back; the jolt runs up my arms into my heart. The fish jumps, runs a few yards, jumps, runs, circles the boat as I swing the rod tip around the stern to follow. And here (for this, as you may have noticed, is not a fishing story in any conventional sense) I must pause to sort out the audience. If you've fished, at least if you've fished for smallmouth bass, you know that electric thrill, the intimate connection with some primitive other. Playing a strong fish, I silently thank God for this moment. Not a prayer to land it, not anymore. Losing a big one is sure to drag out an "Oh, *shit!*"—God understands—but it's the experience that lingers, not the outcome. In memory, even if not at the exasperated moment, the experience is complete if you clearly see the fish. At Pine Terrace, when I was about fourteen, I hooked a pike far larger than any we ever caught there—ten pounds at least, going by fish that size I caught later. I'm glad it got off, because we'd have kept it. I wish to this very day, over forty years later, that I'd gotten a look at it. When I was in my twenties, I dragged to the surface of a deep Canadian lake a mighty lake trout. It fought like a log. Twenty, twenty-five pounds, bigger than any fish I've caught in the thirty years since. Do I regret not getting it into the boat? I'd have kept it. Eight, ten nice messes!

The writer Ernest Hemingway would have said, some time ago, shut up about it. The experience is incommunicable. Talk guts it. The writer William Faulkner would be going on at great length about how mystical it all is, and loving the animal you kill. Which, with reference to the hypothetical deer lying dead at my feet, I have some difficulty understanding. If I were a Plains Indian and it were a bison, certainly. And we, my son and I, do truly love these fish. *That's why we put them back in the water.*

The reader who's never fished, meanwhile, has been waiting her—let's say, not of course to stereotype anybody—turn with little patience. *"Men"*, she says. What a lot of fuss over a romanticized adrenaline rush. Which you go to great trouble and expense to bring about, which lasts two or three minutes, which arrives on no schedule at the end of an hour or more, maybe, of fruitlessly, repetitively, *mindlessly* hurling three-eighths of an ounce of metal and plastic into the water and dragging it back out again. Not to mention the basic mismatch involved—you'd think you were going after a grizzly with your bare hands. You come home all breathless and triumphant, telling me you caught an *incredible bass! Over four pounds!* To your what, one- seventy-five? And where is it, by the way?

Swimming around in the river. And it really was an incredible bass. The rush, lasting more like ten minutes on that occasion, was indeed intense. Maybe it came at the end of a slow hour—I no longer clearly remember—but surely not as slow as the hour spent in line at Disney World. The rush at the end of the line is guaranteed, of course. You've had it before, the very same one: Disney World, the McDonald's of adrenaline. You forked over a few dollars more for your day at the park, I'm guessing, than we for our day on the river. And at no time during that day were you connected with the wild—the wild without, the wild within. To your soul, that is what matters.

And as for four pounds vs. one-seventy-five, what a cheap shot. Cheap, that is, unless you *consciously* reject play—sport—as an integral part of a healthy adult life.

Unconscious reasons for rejecting it might be:

1. Your mother was (check as many as apply) a deer/trout/ bass/football/basketball/baseball/hockey/golf/tennis/ bowling widow, and never let anyone forget it.

2. Your father/mother never forgave you for not becoming the football star/Olympic gymnast that he/she never forgave him/herself for not becoming.

3. Your wife ran off with her tennis instructor.

4. Your husband, forty-plus weekend warrior, spends half his weekends in the emergency room.

5. The greed and hypocrisy of professional athletes makes you want to gag.

6. The greed and hypocrisy of big-time college sports programs makes you want to gag.

7. Bobby Knight.

8. Death threats leveled at critics of Bobby Knight by supporters of Bobby Knight.

What's missing here, of course, is adulthood. Try ultimate Frisbee, outdoor chess, slow-pitch softball and playground basketball. Italian-speaking Saturday morning soccer games. Elderly foursomes on the golf course or the tennis court. Division III college football, with a few hundred fans and no television cameras, coached by gentleman-teachers. A former student of mine, a single mother, bonding with her son on the riverbank. Us on the river this morning, one grown man and one growing nicely, thank you, playing with the fishes.

And since fishing is play, it has rules. At 175 pounds, using a 50-pound-test hand-line, I could drag this bass I'm playing into the boat in a few seconds—so I don't. I handicap myself by using a limber rod weighing two or three ounces and six-pound-test line. The fish has every chance. At the same time, the tackle mustn't be *too* light, lest the fish play itself to near-fatal exhaustion—or, having snapped the line, swim off with the lure in its mouth. What we seek here, as in every aspect of life, is balance.

The fish, of course, was not asked if it wanted to play. An argument more cogent when applied to that beloved (in the Faulknerian philosophy) deer whose antlers are now a coat rack; true, nevertheless. *Balance:* between unbending ethical duty on the

45

one side, indulgent delight on the other, a middle ground.

In due course I do, with Jeremy wielding the net more neatly than I did, land this fish. Release is delayed slightly, by twenty or thirty seconds, because I take a notion to measure it. Why? Well, because it might be fifteen inches, at which length it would be designated by Pennsylvania standards as a "big bass," legally keepable in "big bass waters." In my journal I note the number caught from twelve inches up; of those fifteen and up I make specific note, and tally them at the end of the season. If this were a really big fish I'd weigh it as well; our record is four pounds five ounces, with a rousing "Great catch!" awaiting anyone who breaks it.

Fifteen and a quarter inches by the tape. I ease it over the side, in a second or two it's gone. It might behoove us to think about what we're releasing, what hanging onto.

four

Hope

We reach the lower end of the island, paddle across to try the pool just below. This has to be the most heavily fished spot on our route; on weekends when the water is higher, we see boats anchored in there as often as not. Boats powered by outboard motors, free to go anywhere there's water enough to float them, and so they do: churn their way up to this hole, throw in a dozen casts, off again to the next. Only the river doesn't work that way. On the big windy Canadian lakes for which they're equipped, yes: point to rock pile to weed bed works. Here, though, what you need to do is drift through productive stretches of water, pick up the pace a little—or just take it easy and bird-watch—through the slower ones. But with five or ten thousand dollars invested in what you're sitting in and powered by, you're not going to drift. You want to use all that muscle. So half the time, running from this putative hot spot to that one, you're not even fishing. Which is what over-reliance on technology can do for you.

Rarely do we see anyone catch a fish here; we don't ourselves, but then we have nothing invested in it. After only a minute or so we push on across the river—back to the landing side—and put ashore on a gravel bar. Just above, in the foot of the riffle sweeping down past the island, we've caught fish. And it's time to get our feet wet, anyway. We both wade in knee-deep, Jeremy, since I caught the larger and more recent fish, in the better spot upstream. The water's a little warmer than the air, maybe seventy-five degrees, luscious against my calves. This is the beginning of a baptism which will end in total immersion. On his third cast, Jeremy misses a nice strike; or rather, since he struck right back, the fish missed the lure. Too bad but okay; we landed our first two, and never catch half the fish we raise. Time for breakfast now. I lift the ice chest out onto the gravel, Jeremy collects the cushions, and we feast on bagels and orange juice. As we eat, a mature bald eagle, white head and white tail, flaps out of one of the big oaks near the foot of the island, circles the island, disappears over the water on the far side. This summer we've seen this bird or one like it more times than not, and young ones also. Nice sighting today, a sign of good river health.

Hope is the thing with feathers, the poet said, which maybe is why I start thinking now about prospects for the day. Two nice fish and a third raised this early, with nearly all the best water ahead—not bad at all. Our record for most keepers in a day—something else we haven't released, most this, biggest that—is thirteen. Could be. Anything's possible. Hope, though, hope if it gets greedy, can carry you down the river ahead of yourself. Hope's shadow is attachment to outcomes.

We clamber into the canoe, which rocks as we get ourselves balanced, paddle back over near the far shore, and fish. The river here, a few hundred yards wide in this stretch between islands, is like a long lake; if I didn't give us a push between casts, we'd just sit. Cast, paddle, cast. Time passes, but not as it does in the other world. We are—for who knows how long?—outside time; fishing as Zen. Until:

"Hasn't it been awhile?"

Jeremy is correct. Nothing, at least as a participant in a fishing tournament would gauge it, is happening.

"Maybe we need current." Which soon picks up; I can put the paddle down and let us drift, but still—and we're halfway to the next island now—nothing. So much for records, it looks like. Not that it's been all *that* long; we weather slow patches, not as during Jeremy's fishing childhood, routinely, only . . .

Only here within hailing distance is a fisherman standing waist-deep in the river, well out toward midstream. No boat; he must have found an access, invisible from here, across the way. He calls out to us, his voice carrying easily across the water, "How'd you make out up there?"

"A couple."

" I caught five right here. Up to seventeen inches."

I cannot quite bring myself, or actually—for what's the point of this enterprise but to discover and tell truth?—let's scratch the *quite*, to, holler back a congratulatory "Wow, that's amazing, what are you using?" We wave in reply. On down we go.

A little later Jeremy says, "So what do you think?"

"Didn't see a stringer." Which I'm pretty sure I would have, trailing downstream from his belt, if he'd had one.

"That's good, anyway." It is—we're prepared to forgive fellow catch-and-releasers a great deal, even success. But *that* much success? Jeremy adds, "Did you believe him?"

Did I believe him? A question with no easy answer. The guy was fishing an underwater lure—a jig, I thought I saw—which doesn't work as well on this river as our top-water prop baits. We know this because we've fished with friends who believed in jigs, stayed with them for futile hours while nice fish rose to our surface lures. We've even seen one, a dedicated bait fisherman, repeatedly get skunked using live crayfish—along with hellgrammites, the premier smallmouth bait. As for catching five keepers in one spot, we've done that once in seven or eight years: not here, either. So did I believe him?

1. It happened exactly as he said, the lucky son of a . . . gun. (He did, after all, put his fish back.)

2. He caught five bass, four in the eight-inch range—small fish are attracted to jigs—and one of fourteen or fifteen inches which he estimated—a tad high. Hey, who doesn't?

3. He caught approximately five bass—like three or four.

4. He thought he had five strikes. Three of them were rocks.

5. He was skunked and frustrated. Invented five bass as a move in the eternal fisherman's game: one-upmanship.

"He probably caught something," I say. "Who ever knows? Let it go; float away down the river."

With apologies to all who are good and true: pro athletes stretch with one hand for the ball, the other for the bucks. Politicians waffle. Fishermen lie. A popular brand of fishing scale is called the DeLiar, and much good it does. They lie by omission and commission, by skewing the context, they hedge, exaggerate, prevaricate. To fellow fishermen about what they caught, where they caught it, what they caught it on. About what they caught, almost caught, would have caught if they had any luck but bad, to fellow fishermen, to their work-mates, wives, children, themselves, and God. Why? Because the human male is a woefully fallen being? A rag doll washed haplessly onto the rocks by flood tides of testosterone? Because, besides being a fisherman himself, he runs a bait shop, a boat rental, a fishing resort, and truth is bad for business?

The first time Keith and I went to the Jersey Shore, we rented from Bobbie's Boats. Bobbie was in fact an individual of the female persuasion: attractive, hardboiled, hard drinking, a subspecies common to waterfronts. To catch weakfish, she told us, you need grass shrimp—lots of grass shrimp at five dollars a quart, with which you not only bait your hook but chum to draw the fish in. (The big party boats anchor in a hole and chum by the cubic yard.) We bought shrimp, we chummed, and we bait-fished. Started catching fish. At some point I wondered: if these weakfish are active and ravenous predators, as their reputation and current behavior suggest, why wouldn't they take lures? I put on a jig, a fifteen-center, with which I could cover more water. It was more visible. I caught *more* fish. When we told Bobbie, she had the grace to look slightly sheepish. She said, "I can't tell people that."

Brochures for fishing resorts lie—in keeping with the field of endeavor, *outrageously*. Anyone who goes to a resort based solely on the text and the fish pictures in a brochure is crazy, as we, having done

51

it a couple of times, are in a position to know. Not that I would ever accuse anyone of violating the truth-in-advertising law—heavens no. What constitutes "great fishing" is of course purely a matter of opinion; doubtless, anyway, somebody had some sometime. Somebody staying at the resort caught those lunkers in the brochure, too. Ten years ago, maybe. At the end of four thousand man-hours of weary pounding, maybe. But then what is truth?

At fishing resorts, time collapses. The proprietor will tell you fifty fish stories in an hour, every one of them true. They sound like they all happened last week, instead of during the twenty-four years he's owned the place, but what is truth? The man's motives, anyway, are not purely economic. He knows what fishermen live on: not beer, beef jerky, granola bars, but hope. The thing with feathers.

When you lose hope—when you're stuck somewhere for a week with nothing to do but fish, hopelessly, you die inside. Your soul shrivels up, and nothing will revive it but getting back to sweet home waters. We learned about that at Crotch Lake, a lovely nine-mile impoundment in southern Canada for which we came to invent other names. Crotch Lake snuck up on us. I went one year in May with my father, just for a couple of days, and had pretty decent fishing for smallmouth bass. Then in early July with the whole family; the fishing was far from great, but there were other things to do, day trips to Kingston, so it didn't really close in on us. Jeremy and I went out one day with a guide (*he* caught three or four walleye; we caught one or two between us), and I asked him what single week of the summer was consistently the best. Last of July and first of August, he told us, and added that last summer, fourteen hundred walleye had been caught from his boat. At *least* fourteen hundred. That did it. We booked, just the two of us this time, for a week in fisherman's hell. Lacking only the sign over the office door: Abandon All Hope, Ye Who Enter Here.

In this particular manifestation of Inferno there are, of course, fish and rumors of fish. If nobody ever caught anything, we could all just hang the proprietor in effigy and go home. The way you catch these fabled walleye is to bait a jig with an earthworm, sink it to the bottom of the lake, and twitch it up. But not just anywhere in the lake; in certain spots about twenty feet deep which you locate with your electronic depth finder. Which we, being incorrigibly low tech, don't own and don't care to. So if we find the fishing less than satisfying, it's our own damn fault? A view the proprietor, a coldly jovial man, does little to discourage. A view which also runs hard aground on the facts. In this heavily fished lake they've introduced what they call a slot system, meaning that walleye in the eighteen- to twenty-four-inch range, prime breeding size, must be released. The problem is that the fish that people catch almost all run smaller—mostly a lot smaller. Mostly—there's no lower size limit—*miniscule*, like (a walleye is a slender fish) twelve inches. And even the high-tech experts, masochists who've been coming here for ten or twenty years, are catching very few of these infants. One morning we go out with yet another guide, the first guide's cousin, thereby transforming ourselves into Experts for a Day. And catch what—one, two? I could look it up, but I don't care to.

Of the days of my fishing life, I have spent seven with professional guides; two by myself on the Lake of the Woods for muskie; these two with Jeremy on Crotch Lake; and three with Jeremy on Lake Kesagami, a genuine fly-in hotspot in upper Ontario which, the week we were there, was mostly shut down by bad weather. (We're going back next year, though—we're hopeful.) These jaunts had a number of features in common—first and strikingly, a dearth of memorable fish. On Lake of the Woods I did see a muskie. On Kesagami, Jeremy did catch a couple of ten-pound pike. However, as the Kesagami guide put it: "I can take people to the good places, but I can't make the fish bite." Fair enough; an assessment in the light of which we, as a society, might well look at our reliance on experts—doctors, lawyers, financiers, technicians, gurus of all stripes. Only . . . .

Reputable stockbrokers do not invest their clients' money for their own profit. Reputable therapists do not use their clients as sounding boards for their own issues. So why do fishing guides fish? A muskie fishing trip that produces one muskie is a raving success; there's a fifty (sixty?) percent chance that the guide will be the one to catch it. We didn't care all *that* much about Crotch Lake's pan-sized walleye, but watching the guide catch them was perhaps less of a thrill than we'd bargained for. Why do guides fish? Because they can't help themselves. With a dry line, what have you to hope for?

Of the four nice pike our guided party caught on Kesagami, the guide caught three. With a young angler in the boat? The last he took by trolling straight astern, between our two lines. He had on a jig on this occasion with no wire leader; one touch of a tooth would have sliced the line, he fretted about losing the fish—his one thousand four hundred seventy-third big one, roughly speaking—but he didn't. I netted it deftly and got it off the hook and safely back into the water. And I don't want to sound harsh. This was a kind old man working for a pittance, twelve dollars an hour for a ten-hour fishing day. He offered Jeremy his rod when the fish got on, with no way of knowing that, of course, Jeremy doesn't do that. Hope was what he was selling for his modest fee; the more lines in the water, the *more* hope. Lines in the water, tales in the air: Right here last week, two years ago, we caught . . . . And fishing stories are fun, true enough. Annotated fishing maps are useful. Yet it's well to remember the *source* of hope: not the guide, not the expert, not the guru. The water itself. Next time we come to Kesagami, we'll fish alone.

Our Crotch Lake guide, meanwhile, tells us a wonderful story about a huge walleye attacking a small hooked walleye. It was incredible! It must have weighed ten pounds! In this way he makes amends for the miserable walleye fishing—which, in itself, need not have been a problem. There are lots of bass in the lake, as I know from that first trip in May, and we do know how to fish for them, but they're not biting either. Not at dawn, not at dusk, not at any hour in any of the bays marked B for Bass on the chart so thoughtfully provided by the proprietor. Which leaves pike, a true game fish, and the one we were most interested in to start with. Crotch Lake is mostly open and rocky, but there are a number of shallow, weedy bays marked P for Pike. In such places, though the larger fish tend to scatter into deep water in the summer, you ought to be able to catch smaller ones in plenty. We know how to fish for pike—by casting spoons or other shiny toys over weed beds. It doesn't work.

So get up early, troll along shores marked W for Walleye. Nothing—maybe one strike. Cast the bays for bass. Nothing. Go in for breakfast. Pound the weed beds all morning for pike. Nothing. Go in for lunch, promise ourselves we won't go back out till suppertime, because it's getting hot as hell. But there's nowhere to walk, nothing to do, how many games of Othello can you play? And we're paying an extravagant rental fee for the boat and motor that are sitting out there at the dock. Back out by two, the air flat, heavy, eighty degrees on the water, pound for pike, nothing. We put on little spinners, try for yellow perch. Catch one or two, panfish worth fishing for with a fly rod if you can catch fifty in an hour or if you're hungry. We are—for something else. Do it again the next day. The next. The next. Almost without hope, but not quite, and that's the worst of it. The atheist on Sunday takes his ease in the back yard with the *Times* and the barbecue. The wanderer in the dark night of the soul . . . casts, casts, casts for a God who gives no sign. Except perhaps this poem, which rose one day like a dead carp to the surface of my mind:

> No fish. Last night from
> the dead lake upstream drifted
> clouds of emptiness.

The fishing at Crotch Lake makes us crazy. Jeremy, because he's thirteen years old at the time, visibly crazy, which is to say that while I'm up in the kitchen preparing supper—typically an Epicurean feast consisting of canned hash, white bread, and chocolate chip cookies—he's down on the dock. Fishing. He casts a small pink-headed jig, our "hot perch lure," again and again over the weeds. Every day for a week. Maybe he catches a perch or two; one could, theoretically, catch pike in such a spot; and we know bass hang out there at times, because I caught some in May. Ultimately we learn that they still do. On our last morning a girl of about eight, who had arrived perhaps half an hour earlier, drops a hook baited with a worm into the water. Within five minutes she pulls out a sixteen-inch bass. *Five minutes. On a worm.* And drags it around the dock for God and everybody to see as if it was some kind of big deal.

When the end finally comes, when I pay our bill, the proprietress does not ask how the fishing was, or hope we had a good time. Yet as we drive out, we see forest behind the resort being cleared, and that tells a tale: they're putting in a nine-hole par-three golf course. A restaurant. *Great fishing and more*—the brochure we receive several months later informs us. *Recreation! Fine dining!*

That splendid example of resort-speak alone, however, was more than we cared to swallow.

Yet Crotch Lake taught Jeremy something he needed to know—and reminded me: there are times when skill does not avail. And human will *never* avails. Your desire will not move one fish one inch toward your hook in a lifetime. Keep your hook in the water, merely, and let it go. Accept what the day brings, remembering above all that your next strike is not owed you; it's a gift. Which is not to denigrate the value of good old common sense, about which we learned something also: do not go twice to Crotch Lake.

This morning on our home river, the sun breaks through the mist. It's going to be hot. Jeremy looks wilted and I feel that way—could we actually go all the way down from here, another five or six hours, without raising another fish? Nobody actually says "Crotch Lake," the direst shorthand in our lexicon; a grimy cloud hanging over our heads. Pretty much the only cloud. If that thirty percent chance for a thunderstorm comes off, it won't be for hours yet.

Jeremy says, knowing there's no answer, "Do you really think that guy caught five bass?"

"Hope so," I say. "If he did then, why shouldn't we later?"

Jeremy states the painfully obvious: "Because they were biting then." And adds, "He was fishing a jig. We got any?"

"Sure."

Not that we use them from one trip to the next, but fishermen tend to carry along everything they ever caught a fish on. We've caught catfish on jigs, once in a great while. But with the sun this high? Jeremy dithers. I keep casting with such attention as I can muster. The head of the second island grows nearer. Finally he shrugs. "Pretty shallow."

Which makes the most basic kind of good sense. Cast a jig over a rocky riverbed only three or four feet down, you're going to hang it up. Then you have to back the canoe around, paddle hard against the current to get an upstream angle on it. That or break it off, and not that the fifteen cents matters, but you're tying on a new one every ten minutes. That'll send the H/FR, Hassle to Fish Ratio, into the red zone in no time.

The other, more fundamental reason to stay with the prop bait is that we know it works. Experiment, yes, when intuition urges. It was intuition that told me to try jigs for weakfish at the Jersey Shore. Intuition told me to try these surface lures, carry on with them in bright daylight when, according to all the conventional wisdom, you ought to go deep. Only in this stretch of this river, there's no *deep* to go to. A few holes, maybe ten or twelve feet, but those have never been productive; the fish hang out in riffles and on flats above riffles in two, three, four, or five feet of water. So why wouldn't a feeding bass rise to a crippled minnow a foot or two over its head? Especially since bass are sight feeders, as the relative failure of bait fishing demonstrates, and ought to be able to see a prop bait thrashing the surface like a little motorboat from much farther off than any jig. And in fact, they see them at such a range that one person tossing short casts to each side can catch nearly as many as two. They see them and come to them at once, hence ninety percent of strikes in the first few feet of retrieve, and at any time of day. One bright afternoon a few years ago we were wading a flat and saw, in the shallow water thirty feet ahead, a flurry and commotion. "Carp," I ever-so-wisely said. Jeremy cast to it anyway and landed a magnificent bass, nearly eighteen inches—the biggest any of us had caught at that time.

Scarcity makes people desperate—naturally enough when it's real scarcity of something that matters. Otherwise, what we're talking about is greed. Greed causes corporations to lay off workers while offering fat stock options to the fat cats on top. To pollute rivers because that's the cheapest and easiest way, and after all, they have to be responsible to the shareholders. And greed, or the greed-scarcity model, causes fishermen to lie. In tough times, to flop about haplessly like a banked carp. The choice ultimately, on a hot forenoon when they're not biting, when the afternoon stretches out ahead into the foothills of eternity, is between flailing and faith. And what feeds faith is memory. This is not Crotch Lake. It's our home river which always, sooner or later, has given to us of its riches. Then too, look: limpid stream, wooded hills, not a soul in sight. "It's important to remember where we are," I say, remembering a time when I said that to my father and what he thought I meant was, "Be sure and take bearings so you don't get turned around." We were fishing on Shoal Lake, a Canadian monster of points and bays and islands. Here, unless we lose ourselves in our minds, there's nothing to fear. The river, which flows one way, will take us home. On down we go, in hope.

five

Loss

On the flat above the second island I get a strike. It comes when I'm not expecting it, the prop bait halfway in, at the end of a long drought. I strike late, way too late, and miss badly.

"Did you feel it?"

"No, go on, cast."

Which is our protocol: a fish that never felt the hook might still be in a biting mood. Now and again, in fact, one will take two or three whacks on a single cast. Jeremy, a fine caster, drops his lure on the spot; predictably, nothing happens. A smallmouth bass chasing minnows is here and gone, which is why casting to feeding swirls rarely works either. When it does, nothing's more satisfying—that sense of a skillful practice, of working the laws of cause and effect. A trout fisherman who's matched a hatch of aquatic insects with the pattern of his fly, who casts to a boil and sees his fly sucked under, is standing in his Gore-Tex waders at the gates of paradise. So with us, although—that trout angler would say—in the crudest sense, because a bass on the prowl will smash any old gewgaw you throw at it.

"Damn, I screwed it up. Looked like a nice one, too."

"You can't always tell." Which is kind, and true — a twelve-incher can move a lot of water. But still. I had an opportunity to which I did not respond; that easy fly ball landed two steps behind me. Ed the Unready. "The readiness is all," Hamlet's line from Act V when at last he can do what he has to. Shake it off, as athletes say. Learn from it. Wake up.

Jeremy is wide awake five minutes later when he in turn gets a nice hit, but the fish just misses. It happens. The jaw of a smallmouth bass, I read somewhere, is not really designed for a vertical rush to take food off the top — how many times did it have a chance to in the course of evolutionary nature? Until we got into the act with our prop baits. Then, just a few casts after that, he gets a hell of a hit, reacts sharply, and this fish is on. Right away it jumps, it's a beauty. Plunges, the drag runs, again it jumps. A third time, and damn it! The lure flies clear.

Arggh!

Bloody hell!

Finally some action, and nothing to show for it.

"Tough luck," I say. "Sixteen inches easy."

"You think?"

"Sixteen anyway." The mate of that dock fish from Crotch Lake, which did not get off. But river fish fight harder, and the weight of the lure, unlike a baited hook, gives them the leverage they need to flip it out on the jumps. The way we fish, we raise more, miss more, and lose more than most. A high-risk angling life.

"Maybe I didn't keep the line tight."

"You kept it tight. It just happened." And then, because we've come to another fork in the road, "Which way do you want to go down?"

The main flow of the river runs to the right of the second island. At the upstream end the water drops off the flat into a turbulent riffle which, though, is deep enough to navigate safely if you pay attention. For a hundred yards it flows too fast to fish—bass don't hold in the heaviest water—then eases back to a nice drift which keeps on all the way down. The fishing there is rarely fast, but we've gotten into some nice ones over the years; three years ago, my father caught an eighteen-incher there. Getting down to the left would require a hike, dragging the boat over fifty yards or more of rocky shoals. Below that is a rock-studded pool, often productive, then a slow stretch running most of the length of the island. It doesn't look like much, but it's produced as many as seven or eight keeper strikes, and it was here that our friend Ron, formerly Jeremy's teacher, caught a twenty-inch bass weighing over four-and-a-quarter pounds. Two-thirds of the way down, a creek enters the river, a trickle poking out of the undergrowth whose existence we had never suspected. Then last summer the fringe of Hurricane Dennis dropped six inches of rain onto the Susquehanna Valley and gouged the mouth of that creek bed to a width of thirty feet. We landed the canoe on a brand new bar jutting forty feet into the river at right angles to the flow, rock over silt, and walked into what might have been a jungle realm. On each side, ten-foot vertical banks. Ahead, the way blocked by a tangle of large downed trees. Pythons twisted about the branches would hardly have looked out of place. And then when we returned at the beginning of this summer, the bar was gone. Hardly anyone goes down this side. We may be the only ones who ever saw it.

Jeremy shrugs, not much caring, and points left.

If he'd landed that fish, the tenor of the day would be entirely different. Losing a nice one on a slow day can spoil your mood for an hour—if nothing else happens in that hour. Losing a big one sinks into your soul. I have lost eleven big fish in my life, every one of which I remember as if it were yesterday:

1. That pike I never saw in Lake Henry, a lake in the Star Lake chain in Minnesota. The first and, in memory though not in pounds, the biggest of all.

2. A miss, not properly a loss, but it feels the same: a mighty surface strike from a largemouth bass, one pitch-dark night on Star Lake.

3. A catfish in the Blue River. I was old enough to be fishing some fifty yards from my father then, and I hollered over—I'd seen a flash of the fish—that it was a carp. I knew at some level even then that it wasn't. A beautiful channel cat, bigger probably than any I ever landed.

4. The huge lake trout that I dragged to the surface of Muncho Lake in the Northwest Territories.

5. A weakfish that dragged my rod over the side off the Jersey Shore.

6. Another, that same day, which got off my jig after I'd played it a long time.

7. A third, the following year, which came up beside the boat with the small weakfish I'd hooked in its jaws.

8. A smallmouth bass, the first big one I ever saw on this river, on a trip one fall day with Jeremy's twin brother. I hooked it underwater, on a Mepps spinner, and couldn't move it at all. Finally it jumped and shook the hooks out.

Who knows?

9. A smallmouth that went deep, could not be moved, never showed.

10. A smallmouth which, as we went down quickly in the current, grabbed my prop bait and ran away upstream with the line singing out against the drag. I clambered out into knee-deep water, leaving Jeremy to manage the canoe, and hung on until it came off, a long way up the river.

11. A smallmouth I hooked while wading a shallow flat and which for a time I thought was a muskellunge. Until it jumped and threw the hooks.

Every one of those fish now swims in the River of Lost Dreams, and there will swim when all earthly rivers run dry. What redeems loss is the grace of a life lived abundantly. Whatever is lost will in some form be found—in time, in the drift of a canoe on sweet waters. Loss of more than fish:

On the second day of that first trip to Jersey, I foolishly leaned my old spinning rod, line baited with grass shrimp trailing into the water, against the gunwale while I cast with another rod. My old rod, with which I'd caught almost all the big fish I've ever caught, the only object other than this canoe which had, for me, any value other than monetary, leapt over the side in an instant. I leapt in after it. Stretched for the handle. Missed it by six inches. Gone.

Fishing one day on the West Branch with Gregory, Jeremy's twin, I hooked a big fish that ran away up the river. The canoe was sliding down in the current a few yards off a marshy shore, the line singing off the reel. No way could my son, about eleven then, work us in from the bow. With paddle in one hand, rod in the other, I managed to shove us a little closer, clambered out at severe hazard to the boat and its cargo. (Yes, of *course* Gregory was wearing his life jacket.) I sprinted to the upstream end of the weed point, reeling all the while. Ultimately I caught the fish, a 43-inch muskellunge; the biggest fish I've caught in my life to this date. But I never saw my paddle again.

One day, out alone on the river in the canoe, I attempted an injudicious turn in a shallow riffle. The canoe tilted past the point of no return. On my right wrist I was wearing an L.L. Bean field watch with a metal band—a band whose safety catch was defective; whose catch, for months, I had known to be defective, but had done nothing about. Instinctively I shot my right hand to the bottom, a foot or so down, to steady the boat. Rolled out of it, saved my tackle—but my watch was gone. The river, by the time I saw my bare wrist and looked, had taken it down and away, into some crevice where, until the battery died, doubtless it kept perfect time.

One day four of us set out down the river in two canoes. Perry— a friendly acquaintance at the time, a friend later with whom we swamped the rowboat—and I went down the left side of the first island, the picturesque and fishless side, and not five minutes down I threw my plug into an overhanging tree. Embarrassing, especially as I was by far the more experienced fisherman. It was an old-fashioned floating/diving contraption, a crude minnow imitation called a Midge-oreno, which I wanted back, so I handed my rod to Perry and set about paddling back up. The water there was deep, the current just negotiable upstream. After a strenuous minute or two we arrived at the branch and I wrapped my arm around it, with the notion of holding the canoe in place while I disentangled the lure. Only the canoe began floating out from under me. I clutched. Leaned. A higher branch scraped my glasses off my face into the water. My astigmatism is such that when I look at the full moon with bare eyes, it resembles a football. I saw the river anew that day.

On our next-to-last day on Lake Kesagami, just the two of us in the boat, we stopped on the sheltered side of Big Island to cook shore lunch. We had no fish, because the wind had blown too hard to catch any, but potatoes and onions deep-fried over a hot fire (attention, shore-chefs: they're done when *dark* brown) were a treat anyway. By the time we ventured around the point into open water, the lodge just visible a couple of miles away, the wind was blowing sixty miles an hour with gusts to seventy-five or more—the low edge of hurricane force on the Beaufort Wind Scale. Our outboard motor died. We rode waves six or seven feet high, trough to crest, to a boulder-strewn shore a mile and half or so down from the lodge; clambered out and into the bush as that wind hammered the boat onto Precambrian granite. No thought of rescuing any gear—we were glad enough, at the end of a mile-an-hour trek through spruce and alder thicket, to have saved ourselves. Only: in that boat was Jeremy's prized fishing cap, which he'd been wearing when he caught every large fish in his life—which, alone of what he owned, he valued beyond its price. When he went back the next morning with one of the dockhands, he recovered four of our five rods. Four of our six reels. Not the tackle box, containing lures, tools, camera. Not one of the boat bags. Not his cap.

Today we get out of the canoe and walk it down over the shoal to the left of the second island. Get back aboard and cast all the way down—no luck, and so we can't help wondering what might have happened if we'd taken the other way. As fruitless a train of thought as you can well imagine. Near the bottom of the island we get into the riffle, whack a rock and tilt. I don't believe we ever hit anything there before. No harm done, and we land at the lunch bar without further ado.

The lunch bar, at this time in his life, is Jeremy's favorite place in the world. It's a rocky islet, with scrub willow growing down its spine, just off the foot of the large island. The heavier flow is to the right as you look downstream, merging into the wide main channel; just in the broad angle between island and islet, a swirling pool, five feet deep even in low water. In that pool and in the current below, one day a few years ago, we ourselves caught five bass. At that time it gave us something invariably, redeemed the slowest trip, but since then something about the river bottom, or simply the habits of the fish, has changed. Who knows or ever can know what home looks like to a fish? We throw in a few casts for old time's sake, then sit on our boat cushions and eat—ham and cheese hoagies, bottled iced tea, a cantaloupe, chocolate-coated grahams whose coating, the minute they're out of the ice chest, begins to liquefy. Two men on the river, the wide river sparkling in the sun, empty of all other human life, nectar and ambrosia. Our blood glucose rises. Across the way, a long freight train rattles and rumbles its way downstream. We doff shirts and hats, walk to the water's verge, and . . . .

"I hate wet wading," my trout-fishing acquaintance said. Wading not encased in hip-, waist-, chest-high neoprene, he meant, or old-fashioned sweaty rubber. Wading kid-style—the water sucks your socks out through the holes in the toes of your sneakers, where they waver in front of your feet like pale, blood-gorged leeches. Understandable when what you're talking about is a sixty-degree trout stream; but still, if your objective is to remain dry—

The swivel chair on the deck of your bass boat will keep you two or three feet above the waterline.

Fishing from a pier or a bridge will raise the safety margin to five, ten, thirty feet or more.

There are all sorts of video fishing games out there.

"Take almost any path you please," Melville wrote,

> and ten to one it carries you down in a dale, and leaves you there by a pool in the stream. There is magic in it. Let the most absent-minded of men be plunged in his deepest reveries—stand that man on his legs, set his feet a-going, and he will infallibly lead you to water, if water there be in all that region. Should you ever be athirst in the great American desert, try this experiment, if your caravan happen to be supplied with a metaphysical professor. Yes, as everyone knows, meditation and water are wedded forever . . . . Go visit the Prairies in June, when for scores on scores of miles you wade knee-deep among Tiger lilies—what is the one charm wanting?—Water—there is not a drop of water there! Were Niagara but a cataract of sand, would you travel your thousand miles to see it? . . . Why did the old Persians hold the sea holy? Why did the Greeks give it a separate deity, and make him the own brother of Jove? Surely all this is not without meaning. And still deeper the meaning of that story of Narcissus, who because he could not grasp the tormenting, mild image he saw in the fountain, plunged into it and was drowned. But that same image, we ourselves see in all rivers and oceans. It is the image of the ungraspable phantom of life; and this is the key to it all.

At the end of that story, Ahab harpoons his nemesis. A tangled line pins him to the side of the white whale, his savage twin. The whale sounds. Carries him home.

During the great logging era, around the turn of the last century, they floated mighty log rafts down the West Branch—three hundred feet long by twenty-six wide, a configuration dictated by twenty-

69

seven-foot sluice gates. In the fall of 1937, in honor of their father Vincent, R. Dudley and V. Ord Tonkin built a hundred-twelve-by-twenty-six-foot raft, weighing eighty tons and, in early spring of the following year, undertook to follow the old route. They launched it at Charlie McGee's farm, a couple of miles above McGee's Mills and some hundred-twenty river miles above the pool into which we now stand poised to plunge. The date was March 8, 1938. The river was high then, as it had to be to float such a monster, chocolate brown, and cold, probably less than fifty degrees. The raft floated for six days without incident, all the way down to the stretch we're canoeing today. But on the 14th it grazed or at most struck glancingly a piling of the Muncy highway bridge, a few yards down from where we'll be landing. That in itself cannot explain what happened next, for the crew had over nine minutes to right the raft before reaching the railroad bridge half a mile below. The river bends to the right between the bridges, the current may have dragged the raft off-line, and there may in addition have been some miscommunication between bow and stern rudder as to which span they were aiming for. The raft, in any case, struck hard this time and tilted steeply, sweeping the deck of all but one of the forty-five passengers and crew. Of these, seven, including pilot Harry Conner, drowned in the Susquehanna. Our home waters, which flow into the main stem and thence into Chesapeake Bay, not far from the mouth of the Potomac where I first wet a line half a century ago; waters so sweet and mild today, into which we now sink over our heads. Next I walk to the head of the pool and body-surf down, hands down and belly sucked up as the river shelves. Jeremy goes down three times, and then, our spirits restored, we launch our boat into the current. Back upriver a few thunderheads have built up—no imminent threat, but something to keep our eyes on.

six

Big One

We enter now into a long stretch of lovely water—rocky bottom, gentle current, a few feet deep the whole way across. A place to give ourselves over to the will of the river. Happy memories here, too. The day I lost my glasses, Perry and I were skunked all the way down to the lunch bar—and the other boat, it turned out, had done well. How could I not, half-blinded, have been hungry for vindication? After lunch with a different partner, drifting this water, I caught five fish, though only two keepers; my new partner, triumphant as he'd been above, none at all. Mean-spirited though I surely was on that day, I can't at this distance much blame myself. Clear seeing means everything.

Today, almost at once, Jeremy gets a nice strike and hooks it. There's a flurry at the surface, then the fish jumps clear—smaller than we thought, a bare keeper if that, but it's been awhile, and we're glad to get it in the net. This one gets measured too, for Jeremy's standards are more stringent than any game warden's; eleven and three-quarters inches is just that, a quarter-inch shy of an entry in the logbook. In Pennsylvania you're allowed to compress the tail slightly, which adds a fraction, and doing it that way gives me twelve and a quarter. Back it goes, the third keeper of the day if we're keeping score. "Would it have been any less fun to catch," I ask, "if it *had* been half an inch shorter?" Jeremy's shrug says *yes and no*. I know what the deal is as well as he does: sure we're keeping score. Will we sometime get to where at the downstream landing we could say: "Caught fish. Lovely trip"? Without wanting to add, "How many was that again?"

It seems to me unlikely, for we're men of our time and place; citizens of the country which during the Vietnam War instituted the body count— which said more about the folks with the calculators than the course of the war, even had the numbers added up. And I in particular come of record-keeping stock. Thus I can report with absolute confidence that in 1974, in eleven trips on Kansas waters, my father caught forty-nine crappie, fifteen channel cat, fourteen white bass, four largemouth bass, three buffalo, two sunfish, one drum, and one gar. But anyway we'll have nothing to clean—or bury—at the end of the day, and it's the memories that will linger.

A little way further down I catch, on successive casts, small fish—eight-inchers which we're always glad to see, logbook-size two years from now. Then, at the head of the flat above the third island, Jeremy gets a heavy strike. His rod bends way down. The fish is not moving much, holding on down there as though gathering strength. Jeremy's face is utterly intent, eyes aimed down the taut line to the point, the barely moving point, where it enters the water. We both know that this is the one we want.

The big one can set your heart to battering its way out through your rib cage. Ahab, twenty years after last reading about him, seems to me an obsessive neurotic who throws temper tantrums on a grand scale. It's the great white whale, the big one, that strikes into the deep places of mind and soul. *The Old Man and the Sea:* a story about a hard-luck fisherman with a taste for baseball. About the big one, and that's why it lingers. Maybe it means feeding the whole family all winter, maybe simply the joy of seeing it in the net, seeing it swim away free. Either way, the intimate connection with so large a life, unseen from day to day or year to year, changes you. So you can believe in the Loch Ness Monster—people need to—or, one way or another, you can go fishing.

The big one also can be, is more often than not, a false god. I wrote a novel—entitled *The Big One,* as it happens—about a boy growing up as his grandfather grows down. Also, as it turned out, about big fish as opening a way into the depths, big fish as sops to the ever-ravening ego-ghosts. Toward the end of the story Brian, the grandfather, has seduced his grandson into a sixty-mile river journey that has everyone else frantic, or maybe he's kidnapped him. When they finally stop along the way, and Gramps falls asleep, Eddie goes fishing:

He walked up to the iris bed and watched the old man's chest rise and fall. Back down to the river, rigged his rod with a green and white Torpedo.

The water ran quickly just off the bar, slower and deeper outside, with nothing to indicate structure. Not where he might have chosen, but it felt good to cast—the rod bending back strongly behind his shoulder, whipping the lure twenty yards upriver to a landing three feet from shore. He worked it down, reeling quickly to keep ahead of the current. Nothing; he'd expected nothing there, but the rule was, fish it before you walk in it. He waded out knee-deep now, cast up and five feet farther out. Nothing. Eight feet farther out, ten, working backwards around the clock face until he was fishing straight out and then down. Nothing. He walked up to where his first cast had landed and cast upstream, again near shore, from there. Nothing. And five feet out. And eight.

He saw some slight disturbance behind the plug, ripples as of a small fish nosing at it, and snapped the rod tip back. The Torpedo ran freely across the surface, its rear-mounted propeller-blade whirling; you could hardly call whatever had happened out there a strike, but still it was a sign of life. And Eddie felt a lurch of relief. *There's nothing in the river this far up—* why should words he knew were not true have such power? Yet it seemed he needed proof and proof again.

He'd left his lure sitting for a few seconds and it had drifted down a couple of feet, slackening his line. He reeled up and gave it a twitch, and the river blew up under it. A great, heavy, thwacking splash—as of the largest rock he could lift not hurled into the water, but expelled with force from the bottom. As he braced back against the rod he caught a broad bronzy shining in the foam, a dark tail appeared and was gone again in a heartbeat, then the rod tip bent to the water and line sang off the reel against the drag. The fish, whatever it was, ran with irresistible power a dozen yards upstream, then rose and thrashed at the surface. But all Eddie could see was white water. Then it sank and for a long time, nearly half a minute, lay still down there, unmoving and immovable. Eddie, hauling back as hard as he could without running more line off, thought the line must have caught in a snag, though the bottom had looked clean, and that he was now fruitlessly fighting the river itself. He was shaking, but now he had time to think—muskie? It almost had to be. Unless a big carp, but hooking one on a surface plug would be outlandishly strange. Catfish had been known, rarely, to feed on top, and a big channel or blue cat would fight like that. But the color had seemed wrong.

He was standing in the water a few feet from shore, holding on while his heart and breathing steadied. What he thought he might do, now, was set his rod down on the gravel, wade in, and see if he could retrieve his lure. The water wasn't that fast, probably not more than four or five feet deep, so that, keeping the line in his hands, he could work his way out close and then dive. He had another Torpedo in his box, but he wanted this one. Then, in slow, heavy, pulsing horizontal arcs, the line moved. The fish was there, swinging out and downstream now in open water.

If it went on like that, swam easily and steadily down with the current helping, it would run all the line off his reel in a minute or two. A hundred and twenty-five yards of line, but only six-pound-test, never made for this. His springy rod, weighing not more than two ounces, had been built for playing bass; it was all he could do to land a five-pound carp in quiet water with it. The treble hooks on his Torpedo were constructed of thin wire—every element of his outfit, the whole as strong as its weakest link, small, light, delicate. Meanwhile the fish was surging down the river past him, the line sawing the water only twenty-five or thirty feet out.

As it came opposite he gained a few feet of line. Now, to give it back as grudgingly as he could, he moved with the fish, wading hard and fast with his knees raised high at each step. With his eyes fixed on the moving point where line met water he staggered, fought for balance with the rod bucking in his hands; so then, a little line a fair trade for free movement, worked ashore slantwise—just upstream from the boat, into which, where it jutted into the water directly in his path, he might otherwise have careened.

Gramps' landing net was there in the bow compartment, its handle within arm's reach as he passed. He never thought of reaching. Not enough hands, and whatever he had on, even if he could somehow get it near enough, seemed not something he could net. Not with one hand, holding the rod in the other. Yell for help—a thought from a year ago. Not enough breath. His attention was all on the river outside and the bar below, which extended downstream for maybe forty more yards. Below that the bank rose sheer, and that meant deeper water. Worse, there was a tree down, still rooted and green, a deadly tangle of branches sunk in the river to the tree's full former height. If he got that far with the fish still on he could swim, ride down the current and maybe slow the thing down as a living sea anchor, but to clear the tree by enough to have any chance he'd have to flail like hell for the far shore, one-handed. Moreover, to have any kind of angle on it he would have to commit soon. Almost . . . right now, and at that moment the line stopped, rose, and the fish, only thirty feet from where he stood, jumped all the way out.

It was a bass. It was by far the biggest bass he'd ever seen, or even imagined could swim here in his home river. Now it sounded again, working near the bottom in slow, gut-wrenching jerks. They'd come more than halfway to the fallen tree. Eddie's notion of swimming clear of it now struck him as ludicrous. He might have made it, the water moving slowly here, but the fish could have swung back into the branches as they passed. Even now, if it sensed cover or just happened to go that way, it could be there in a few seconds, and there was not a thing Eddie could do about it.

But the fish jumped again, flailed violently in the air just a few feet farther out. Eddie, as he'd done instinctively the first time, lowered the rod tip. That slackened the line, creating leverage for the plug to be whipped clear. But the aerial jerking on a tight line could snap it like a thread. When the fish cracked back into the water he eased the tip back up and felt it bend. Still there. Again it sounded.

But now, now if it was going to jump, sound, fight in short runs, the battle was on Eddie's terms. Any jump could throw the hooks, or a stressed hook could straighten enough to slip out. If neither of those things happened, if there was no unsuspected knot or fray in the line, in time, keeping steady and alert, he must win. So it happened. Three more jumps, each a little closer; between each, working ever so carefully, he was able to pump in line. At last the fish was swimming in slow dogged circles, in view. It was an incredible fish. The measured eighteen-incher he'd caught just days earlier was nothing like it. Gramps had said that twenty inches was almost the outer limit for smallmouth in the Susquehanna. It went beyond that. The twenty-two-incher he'd seen pictured in the paper, caught where the river flowed through River City? Beyond that. *Beyond.* The Big One.

He had time now to consider what to do, alone with no net. He'd waded out a little way to play the fish without dragging it up against the shelving gravel bottom. It was exhausted, barely upright, swimming in a foot of water almost at his feet; he could see the red flash of gills as the gill covers flared and closed. What he wanted was to hold it in his hand but not lift it from the water. The plug was hanging out of the corner of its jaw, the front treble dangling clear. If he reached for it and it flailed one last time, yanking those hooks into his hand . . . .

But if he didn't, and soon, it might die right there in the edge of the river. He knelt, holding the rod high in his right hand to keep a little pressure on, and caught hold of it by the lower jaw between his thumb and fingers. Now he tossed his rod away onto the bank. It was only a matter of working out the hook, the one hook of the rear treble that had gripped for all that time. A little twist and pull did it, and he tossed the lure away also and walked out deeper, thigh-deep, holding the fish upright between his hands. He held it lightly, head upstream, watching it breathe. It rested there for nearly a minute, then, with slow flicks of its tail, swam down, away toward the middle of the river, out of sight.

Eddie watched it and watched where it had disappeared, and then raised his eyes and looked around, blinking. For all that time he had lived in another world. He waded ashore, picked up his rod, and held the lure in his hand. The engaged hook was wrenched, twisted until it barely resembled a fishhook. He looked back upstream to the boat, to the iris bed where his grandfather still lay. Had slept right through it, and did not know that Eddie was now changed.

What he wished for was that his grandfather would not wake right away, and he got that wish too. An hour to himself to wander up and down the bar, gazing out at the river that had such wonders in it.

Throughout the story, Gramps has been obsessed with catching a huge — hypothetical — muskellunge, the biggest fish in the river. The following day, then, a good many miles on down:

Thirty yards from the boat, in the flat water behind Brian's plug, something rippled the surface. Bulged it. Eddie knew what a big bass following a Torpedo looked like. Nothing like this. Whatever was trailing the Muskie-Kill was four or five feet long. Gramps yanked the lure into a frantic scurry-skitter, the bulge accelerated behind it, and the rod, broomstick-sized and nearly as stiff, bent double.

"Oh Jesus, I've got him!" He struck again. Again as against a rooted deadhead. "Jesus Christ, I've got that son of a bitch good." He stood in the stern, legs spraddled. "Just hold the boat. That's all you've got to do, hold it out here in the middle."

There was little current. The boat was going nowhere except maybe where the fish dragged it, back up the river with the line buzzing off Gramps' reel. Now it rose, fins glinting red-orange in the sunlight, in a hoop-shaped leap. Again, foreshortened, but Eddie, dry-mouthed, had never dreamed such a thing swam in the river.

"Try it. Go on, try anything. I've got thirty-pound line and a foot of steel leader. 4-0 trebles. I've got you, you bastard."

Forty yards out and sideways on, the fish jumped again. Then lay for a moment inert in the water, and Gramps, leaning back against the rod, began pumping it in. "Yes. Oh yes, you're mine. Think you're going somewhere? My wall is where you're going."

"Jesus, how big is it?"

"Four-and-a-half feet. Five. Forty pounds or more. The biggest son of a bitch that ever swam this river, and he's mine."

Twenty yards out the muskie turned and ran back out. Not quite as far. Again Gramps pumped. "That's fine. All the time in the world. Bastard, son of a bitch, you come to me."

A third run, a fourth, shorter. "Wall behind the counter," Gramps said, and for the first time since the fish was hooked, Eddie glanced up at him. "They'll all see him. Make trips to see him. Tell everybody. Come here, baby. Nearly time."

The line sliced the water in a shorter, slower arc. Eddie could see a long gray shadow down there. "Gramps, get the oars in?"

"Do it. You're with me, you're here, you'll tell them. Come here, baby. You want to be famous all over town? All over the state? You're going to be in the paper, babe. On television. You've been discovered."

The fish arced past, barely ten feet out and two down. Eddie saw it plainly now in profile, eye and flaring gill cover. It was nothing like a big bass. It was as long as he was tall, toothed power, too big and fierce and wild to share the boat with. He was scared of it and, as Gramps yanked it back around, sorry for it.

"How are we going to land it?"

"Net. I'll tell you when I want it. Couple more minutes, baby. Ever wonder about life in the fast lane?"

Net it. The net was big enough if the fish swooped headfirst into the middle of it. But . . . .

He looked closely when it swam back past the boat. It was the rear treble hook that gripped it, tight in the corner of the jaw; the forward gang was clear. If your aim with the net was off, if once you'd committed the fish swerved or dived, and those dangling hooks caught the rim . . . .

"Net. Now."

"Let me net it. I've got two hands."

"Boy to do a man's work? Give it to me."

Eddie handed it over and clutched his arms tight across his chest. Gramps, rod high in his right hand and net poised in his left, leaned out—dangerously far out. Then the fish made a little run and he had to set the net back down and reel.

"Come on now, baby. Time's up."

It wasn't only that Eddie had two arms. Seated with his legs spraddled on each side of the middle seat, he had a far better angle. With one hand back near the end of the four-foot handle of the net, the other close to the rim, he could have leaned out with his hand actually in the water, the net still, just submerged. Brian, with both hands for the heavy rod, could then have led the fish straight in, at the last instant laying the line and the dangling hooks safely against the side of its head. Then a quick two-handed twist of the net, laying it flat on the surface, would have trapped the fish head-down, with nowhere to go but deeper into the mesh. Even if Eddie could not by himself have lifted it all the way out and into the boat, he could have held it until his grandfather could help. Brian's angle, though, verged on impossible. The tip of the rod, held one-handed, wavered six feet above the surface. That gave the fish, which was not entirely played out, a little room to maneuver. And Brian had to hold the net by the very end of the handle to have any chance of reaching—in his left hand, and both his arms were wobbly. If he did get the fish in the net and tried to raise it one-handed, a forty-five pound weight at the end of a four-foot pole, his wrist would buckle and he might lose fish and net and all.

He took the net up again. Braced his foot on the gunwale. Reached.

Eddie, leaning back now to balance the boat, watched. The fish was swimming alongside, moving of its own volition, for Brian was in no position now to do anything with the rod except drag it back away from the net. It had practically to swim in by itself. Here it came. Brian shoved the net at it like a man scooping a beer can off the water. The lower rim stayed too shallow and the fish, spooked, dived nearly clear. Just its head went in. The trailing hooks caught. Brian, who seemed not to have seen what had happened, dropped his rod, dropped to his knees, caught the throat of the net in his right hand to draw the fish all the way in. But the fish was anchored. Brian saw now and wrenched the head up and over the gunwale, dragging desperately against what for only an instant was dead weight. Then the fish thrashed, scale and tail and fin, blood, bone, muscle, flying water, the hooks straightened, and it crashed away free into the river.

Brian dived in after it into water over his head, wrapped his hands around the log-thick midsection and scrabbled for a hold further up—gills, eyes, jaws, he'd have given away his fingers. But he was in another country now. The muskellunge swam easily away from between his hands, and down, and out of sight.

Then for a moment Eddie thought his grandfather was going to drown. The old man floundered in the water ten feet from the boat, making no effort to swim. Eddie grabbed for the oars, and it seemed all he could do to get the balky boat in motion. But he brought it alongside and caught his grandfather's wrist in both hands.

"Come on. Gramps, grab hold."

"My luck. Goddamnit."

"Gramps."

He got him to take hold, finally, but there was no way to get him aboard except to draw him along behind, a monstrous sea anchor, into shallow water.

"Come on. Get in."

"Never another chance. One. All you get."

"You sit in the back. I'll row."

He rowed, slowly, staring back at the place. That the river, his river, had that in it. After a time the bridge came in sight, then, a good while later, the landing. That fish. Muskie. The big one, still down there. It would lie still at the bottom for a long time, just breathing. When it was ready, it could eat the biggest fish Eddie had ever caught. He had never felt so happy. When he looked at his grandfather's face, never so sorrowful.

What will men do, then, to catch a big one?

My father, when he was a boy, hooked into a big northern pike. His father was so frantic to land the fish that he grabbed the line and played it in himself. Maybe in nearly eighty years my father has forgiven him, but he has not forgotten.

Suppose, Jeremy asked me, I had a choice: I could have a normal summer on the West Branch and take my chances. Or I could get skunked for the whole season in exchange for a solid strike—with a good chance of catching it, he specified, but no guarantees—from the biggest bass in the river. A bass resembling the one Eddie caught. I would be taking, if I accepted that bargain, what might be called the Muskie Way. A few years ago we'd see a man following that path, trolling muskie lures up and down, up and down; the summer I asked him he'd had, he said, five strikes and caught a couple, one hell of a good year. At the far end of the spectrum is the Bluegill Way: you'll catch lots of fish but never a big fish. I find it hard to picture Coach Knight as a bluegill man; I see him subduing blue marlin. Then the Smallmouth or Middle Way. A hundred keepers in a summer, three big ones; nothing quite like Eddie's fish, more like the one Jeremy now has on, which now jumps, which jerks a prayer into my throat—*Please, God. Please*. It's one hell of a big bass. It looks so fine!

To catch a big one would you:

Use tackle so heavy you can skitter a five-pound largemouth bass across the surface like a minnow? Tournament anglers do that. The longer a hooked fish remains in the water, after all, the greater its chances of getting off. The object is to get the fish into the boat. It's worth money.

Bait your hook with a live baby duck? It's illegal, of course, but it won't hurt the duck—unless that world record muskellunge does happen to go for it. Then, assuming you land that record fish, you're going to have to lie. "I caught it on a . . ." On a lure manufactured by a large company, one known to be generous with its endorsement fees. I don't suppose you'll mind.

Steal a fish off another fisherman's bank line?

Claim to have caught, legally on hook and line, a world record fish you found floating belly up? (Freshly dead, let's hope, for reasons of aesthetics and plausibility.)

Would you do any or all of the above if it was *the* big one?

The big one, in the world of North American freshwater angling, is the largemouth bass that would surpass the record of 22 pounds 4 ounces, caught in Georgia in 1932. That is nearly seventy years ago. Thousands upon thousands of expert tournament bass fishermen have been trying for millions upon millions of man-hours since then, and none of them have come close. Some people think that fish was a genetic freak, that there are no more bass that big. Wouldn't it be a stitch if some kid broke the record with a worm? A couple of kids tossed a worm into a pond in Lawrence, Kansas, and dragged out—it must have been moribund, given the tackle they were using—a world's record buffalo, a rough fish resembling a carp, weighing over fifty pounds. A life-sized model of that fish remains on display on the campus of the University of Kansas, in the natural history museum. For a fisherman, that's about as close to eternal as fame gets.

Given the money that's invested in largemouth bass fishing in this country every year, anyway, whoever catches a twenty-two- pound-five-ounce bass, properly witnessed and attested to, will never have to work again in his life. You think I'm exaggerating? I'm not. This is a country where bass champions win bass boats, sports utility vehicles, five-to-six-figure cash prizes, have their own television programs, appear on boxes of Wheaties. Tackle endorsement contracts alone would offer lucrative opportunities to lie for money. Not lie as to what tackle was involved, for I wish to impugn no one's honor, but—because that fish would likely have hit anything that was dangled in front of its face, definitely have been dragged in by any rod and reel and line stout enough to do the job—lie in the implication that it mattered. And then the personal appearances at malls and car dealerships. The livin's easy . . . .

Jeremy, if he caught the world record bass, would put it back in the water and never tell anybody. I would, too. But not when I was sixteen. Early one August morning when I was two or three years younger than that, my father and I walked the dew-drenched path to Beaver Lake. We had with us a minnow bucket containing a dozen or so leopard frogs that I had caught the previous afternoon. When we got out on the water, we each hooked a frog under the chin and tossed it out without a weight to struggle on the surface—to become what we hoped would be an irresistible surface lure. It was from this lake, the last day of our first trip, that I caught my first big bass on a frog fished underwater. When we fished them that way we would raise them periodically for a breath of air—because a live bait presumably is more attractive than a dead one.

On this particular morning, anyway, within a few minutes I had what remains the most spectacular surface strike of my angling life. When fishing bait, as opposed to the artificial lure with which Jeremy has hooked into a big one of his own, you let the line run out for ten seconds or so before setting the hook. Imagine me, then, at thirteen years old during those ten seconds. The Moby Dick of the mind down there. I struck, the rod bent, the line ran tight between us like the bonds of fate. It sloshed at the surface—the big one in the grip of gravity, too heavy to jump clear. It sloshed, it surged, it came closer . . . it was no bass. It was a bowfin, what we called a dogfish, a predatory "trash" fish two feet long and weighing five or six pounds. Big one—bigger than any bass we could hope to catch. We netted it, heartsick. We slaughtered it savagely, my father sliced its gill rakers and threw it overboard to bleed to death. To bleed slowly to death, as my father later wrote:

> A few minutes later, the shell of the anchored boat
> Transmitted a strange, improbable tapping.
> Useless, unsteered, ultimate swimming
> Had brought up the perishing fish to collide
> With the boat, and weakly collide again.
> For perhaps as long as it took him to die
> My heart tapped a chilly question:
> Was Something, in code, addressing me?

We killed that fish for not being what we wanted. It was for the good of the fishery, we said, not quite in those words, to rid it of undesirable carnivores; acting, thus, in the spirit of those who murder wolves. Salmon fishermen in Nova Scotia loath mergansers, I've been told, the fish-eating ducks which grace our local river. A trout fisherman I know—an artist with a fly rod, stream entomologist, dedicated restorer of habitat—has spoken in my presence of blue herons in language fit to sear the feathers off them. The fish in the water are ours, we seem to think—by divine fiat? If we don't want them we can throw them out on the bank, as many a carp fisherman has, to stink in our nostrils.

I no longer fish with frogs, or live bait of any kind—I prefer not to. On the last trip to Jersey, Jeremy used minnows and grass shrimp, a choice subject to inner debate only. Over the past thirty-five or forty years I've killed no fish in anger—a state of mind I came to earlier in my life than my father, who on the day of the dogfish was in his mid-forties. He'd learned from his own father, maybe, who hated not fish of any sort but snapping turtles—for their predation of baby ducks. So we set bank lines for turtles and finally did catch one; I forget what the scant edible parts tasted like. One day on Beaver Lake, fishing with a minnow, my father hooked a big one:

> It was a twisting, ominous thing
> That my fishline raised through water dimness, up near
> The surface. It shattered *now*
> Into grisly *then*. My nerves spasmed
> As though to trigger a deathshriek
> From a food-thing grabbed by the lizard-fanged antique.

He undertook to slit its throat with his pocketknife, having forgotten that snappers are "tough, very hard to kill," and was lucky to get away with all his fingers. Only after that attempted murder, which in the poem he neglected to mention, did "the turtle clear and diminish, and plunge/To the innocent bottom in algaed innocence."

Not until the summer I was twenty-four, fresh out of the Army, did we begin to restore big fish to the water. I'd read, I think in *Outdoor Life,* about a place called Brabant Island where you could catch big pike and arctic grayling. No luxury lodge this—you brought your own sleeping bags to spread out on the bunks, cooked your own meals. Which appealed on principle—more to my father and me than my mother, I expect, who in our old-fashioned household never got a break from housework—and eased the financial pain. Brabant Island sticks up—not very far up—out of the headwaters of the Mackenzie River, where it leaves Great Slave Lake on its way to the Arctic Ocean. I'd driven up earlier, a solo trek up the Alaska Highway, and met my folks in Yellow Knife—the metropolis of what was then the Northwest Territories of Canada.

During our week at Brabant we caught over four hundred pike, about forty in the nine-to-sixteen-pound range—we kept score starting at nine because eight pounds was our best heretofore—and one, my father's lifetime biggest, of twenty-three. Putting them back was easy. We couldn't have kept more than a few anyway, legally, and what would we have done with them if we had? We did take the twenty-three-pound fish in alive to show off at the dock; I remember clearly the sight of it from above, quiescent in the shallow water, and I hope that in our vanity we didn't kill it after all. By the end of our stay, my father's and my hands looked as if we'd spent the week, gloveless, clearing a pasture of blackberry canes. It was gorgeous, unforgettable pain, the week itself a life-giving experience of abundance. When you've caught that many big fish, you don't have to worry about it any longer. It was a lifelong weaning from greed.

Yet in some strange way, those fish were not big after all; which is to say that except for my father's record-setter, I don't remember a single one of them. We weighed the largest; mine was over sixteen pounds, but I caught so many others close to that size that I now have no memory of the day or circumstances. Ask me about my *other* sixteen-pound pike, though, and I would reply, How much can you stand to know? It came out of the Lake of the Woods a year or two later, on a trip when a fish like that was an event. I had cast a small yellow jig near the shoreline, and the fish hit it almost at once. It swam off slowly, with a power I could not resist, from left to right. In the water near the boat and in the net it looked huge; I was a little disappointed that it didn't weigh twenty pounds. Which in itself is something to pay attention to: that wanting more and yet more, so that what the day and the water give you is never enough.

Ultimately I released that hunger also, along with the fish itself. Mental health, I read somewhere, is devotion to reality at any and every cost. And what reality says is that within the material realm, space-and-time-bound, everything has limits. The carrying capacity of the planet, the oil that remains in the ground, economic growth; the number of walleye in a Canadian lake, the size of the smallmouth bass in a Pennsylvania river. I may already have caught the biggest bass I'll ever catch out of the Susquehanna, but never mind—this one Jeremy has on right now, still on after a third heart-stopping jump, looks fine indeed. Fine enough, when I finally get the net under it, to pull a rousing "Yes!" out of both of us. You might think, going by what you've seen in seafood shops, that you could sum up the difference between a twelve- and an eighteen-inch bass as "more of the same." Not so. A big fish, one approaching the limit for its species and the water it swims in, has a look of great power about it, a power which, if you close the circle by sending it back home, lingers. This fish, my quick work with the tape measure tells me, is a little over nineteen inches long. It's probably seven or eight years old, a great age in the natural world—virtually every robin you saw two springs ago is dead now—and it's rare. We might see two or three fish this size out of over a hundred in a summer.

"Want me to weigh it?" It's a heavy-bodied fish, maybe three-and-a-half pounds; Jeremy's caught one a little longer but more lightly built, so this could well be his heaviest bass ever.

"No, I just want to get it back in the water."

As fish get bigger, time between catch and release becomes more crucial. The canoe by this time has drifted into the shallows at the head of the island. While I was measuring, Jeremy was tweaking the barbless hook out. Now he scrambles out, knee-deep in the river, and lowers the fish in—supporting it between his hands, head upstream. You can revive an exhausted fish by moving it forward and back to get the gills fanning, but this one is breathing on its own and swims off after only a few seconds. We watch it out of sight. And then I offer my son a high five, which stands for what we don't need to say. Every day on the river is fine. Today, though, we've connected with a power of the river, an event on which the day now centers. The morning's frustrations have flowed away, twigs on their way to the ocean.

seven

Home

The third island, in low water, offers options to the fish-starved. The flow in cubic feet per second down each side is roughly the same, but to the right, on the island side of the channel, is a weed-bordered stretch of slack water running the whole way down. On that side the island itself is dense with scrub alder and willow upstream, timbered below, impenetrable; on the left, shelving gravel makes walking easy. So you can drift down left, casting the channel as you go, then paddle back up the slack water on the right side and fish that; or go right, put the boat in at the foot of the island, then walk up and fish the left-hand channel by wading it. Plenty of fish on each side, but who's starving?

When I ask him, Jeremy says, "Let's go left. I want to check out the carp hole." Which reminds us that there's more to a fishing trip than just fishing. The route to the left is marginally shorter, anyway, and we can't forget about the sky entirely. Storms can come up fast and they can raise the hairs on the back of your neck—when you hear that first loud crack of thunder. No reason lightning should strike the water, with high wooded banks on both sides, but still, there you are in your small metal boat. On the trip with our friend Ron, the day he caught a four-pound bass back up beside the second island, we dawdled along without worrying about thunderheads; the fishing was great and we were all good friends. When the first storm hit, we sheltered at the bottom of the flat below this island, then set out on the two-mile run for the landing—a lot of wide, slack, open water down there, and the johnboat with three of us in it went creakily. We were nearly down to where Muncy Creek flows in, still close to half a mile to go, when wind-driven rain caught up with us; in near-darkness I put over to the creek mouth, Ron and Jeremy jumped out and ran for home across the shallow flats while I rowed the lightened boat. That was one glorious day to remember. About storms, though, I remember one when I was out with Jeremy's brother; he was only six. We put in at the foot of this island and sat it out, my son scared and I, holding him tight, trying to muster enough courage for both of us. The canoe was half-full of rainwater after that, the picnic cooler afloat. On that storm, later, I modeled this scene in *The Big One:*

Matt watched the clouds build up, tall thunderheads in the southwest. Toward four o'clock, way off on the horizon, lightning flickered. Still, he reckoned they had time. When Brian got up and returned from the tree which, by the end of summer, at this rate he was going to piss the bark off, Matt caught his eye and pointed. "Getting pretty dark. Maybe we better head on down."

"Muskies hit before a storm. We'll fish it."

"Bass are down. I only raised one little one."

"Bass are a fair-weather fish."

He turned away, scooped up his boat cushion, and went and sat down in the stern of the boat. Matt shook his head. Stared at the sky as he pushed off into the current. Nothing to do now, unless you preferred flailing the water for what would not show itself, but wait.

Nor was there long to wait. By five o'clock the air, which had been heavy and still, stirred randomly in light chilly puffs. For the next half hour these increased in velocity and duration until the air all around them was in motion, a cold gusty wind from the southwest. The sky was dark gray except for a strip of cobalt blue on the eastern horizon. Thunder rolled up behind them. Matt edged the boat closer to shore, the densely overgrown bank of the third and last island; downstream from there was a long riffle, difficult to get through in low water without getting out and towing, then a two-mile pool to the bridge and the landing.

He had little attention to spare now for Brian, still heaving his lure down the wind; wind gusting to forty miles an hour and more, and then lightning hit a tree at the head of the island, not a hundred yards upstream, thunder cracked like doom, Matt's hair stood up under his cap, and the rain came, driving at them in horizontal sheets. Between lightning strikes it was almost dark, the sky blue-black, treetops madly tossed in white electric light and then gone. Matt, head down, rowed like hell until the bow of the boat dug into a mud bank. He shipped the oars and scrambled out, knee-deep in muck with a foot of water on top of it, lurched forward balancing himself against the gunwale, mud dragging at him, sucking his sneakers off, and he leaned in against the bank, his upper body tangled now in grapevines. How high and how steep was the bank? He couldn't see, eyes full of water; he hung onto the bow with one hand, the tough vines with the other—"Come on, get ashore, hurry." When he felt and heard no response, he wrenched his head around full into the wind, and in the next flash caught an incredible glimpse of Brian still with his rod in hand, still reeling, though quickly; he turned back, hanging on for dear life, the boat with his weight out of it and Brian back in the stern afloat again, so that if he let go, the wind would whirl it away down the river, into the dark. Hung on, teeth gritted, head ducked, shut his eyes tight to squeeze the water out of them, and in that instant, as the stern at last heaved up and Brian floundered toward him, he saw with utter clarity, green and gray and red in a field of white light, what the old man was after; it was an image, photographically exact, of the muskellunge mounted in Rick's Bar.

Brian scrambled up the bank and in among densely under-grown alder. Matt looped the bow rope around a cluster of vines, tied it, and followed. There they were, huddled in a tangle of soaked vines, treetops whipping thirty feet over their heads. They were a little out of the wind, rain pooling on them off the trees instead of driving down the open river. The trees here, lower growing than the oaks and willows at the head of the island and on both shores, were unlikely lightning rods. Otherwise, they were not sheltered.

The riffle to the left of the island is deep enough to ride down even in low water. Far left, on the mainland side, is a backwater into which I now shove the canoe; at the bottom end of it, fifty yards down, a big maple with its lowest branches trailing in the current. From above, through the airbound angler's eye, it looks like a place which would have to harbor fish. And in my reference book, in fact, smallmouth are referred to as "contact fish," meaning they like to get next to something. (Which makes them, in that one way, human-like.) A mile or so upstream, a couple of years ago, a tree fallen into the river came to be for us the magic tree; it produced a strike ten trips or more in a row. Over the winter it washed away. But cast to any of the dozen trees that looked just like it? To every one of every year's new crop? Nothing. Work your plug over any number of pockets formed by any number of stones, structure you'd photograph if you were *writing* that bass book? Nothing. Drift or wade a flat with no structure at all? That's where it happens. This river, even as it gives us its gifts, humbles us.

This tree we're drifting down on has to be cast to—obstacles draw bass fishermen as magnets draw iron. To Jeremy it's a point of honor to whip his lure right in under, both because, like Everest, it's *there,* and because he once got a fine strike by doing that— once. Out of how many tries? Not to mention the times when the tree, turned predatory like one of Tolkien's sinister willows, has devoured the lure. That's the way of it in home waters, though: if the fever has got you like malaria buzzing away in your blood, you have to try every spot where you ever caught, lost, or missed a fish, which adds up to practically every square yard of water the whole way down. You could be out there for three days, if not saved by herons, mergansers, kingfishers; by blue wild iris, called flags, in June, in August by purple loosestrife, an invasive weed resembling, in its astonishing beauty, fireweed; by baptismal immersions, good fellowship or solitude, the sufficient riches of a day on the river. Remember where we are: home.

Today's adventure with the tree is something of a wash: Jeremy snakes his cast right in under where he wants it, but nothing rises.

"You *ought* to be rewarded for a cast like that."

"Damn straight," I agree. "Is there no cosmic justice?"

Thank God there's not, though—in just that sense. The skilled casters, gimlet-eyed bargainers at the Counter of Cause and Effect, would empty the river of fish in a season.

And then, wouldn't you know it—I put the canoe across the channel, toss a cast over near the weeds fringing the island. About all you can say of it, considered as an athletic feat, is that it lands on the water; but it draws, instantly, a whacking strike. I hook it, too, the electric thrill running strong up my arms. There was a time, in Jeremy's earlier youth, when if he hadn't been doing well I paid for every fish I caught. There was a day, out with Jeremy's twin, when I tried to coerce the river gods into favoring my young son by putting on an underwater lure, a flatfish, which I thought wouldn't compete. I caught a forty-three-inch muskellunge on it. Now Jeremy grudges me nothing even on bad days, much less this one, and I relax into playing my fish—simply happy. Only the fish is behaving oddly; it seems heavy but jerks back and forth, not swimming in any coherent way. I would now rather not lose this, whatever it might be, without seeing it. Now it comes up into the shadowy verge of view, it looks oddly misshapen, it . . . is *two* bass, one hooked on each treble. Jeremy scoops, lifts, we're both laughing at the crazy wonder of it. Two nice keepers, thirteen or fourteen inches each, to slide back into the water one after the other.

"That's six nice fish for the day. A limit."

"Cool."

One limit between the two of us, that is, as defined by the Pennsylvania Fish Commission in its wisdom: the number of bass that could theoretically be taken out by each angler fishing these waters, without disastrously depleting the population. Here that might be true—though we raise a cheer whenever we see someone put one back. The theory, though, is decidedly rough and ready. We fished the Juniata River one time, south and west of here, drifted ten miles or more of it in the company of three or four other canoes. It was a Saturday, a fishing tournament was going on, and we must have seen a hundred boats. We saw close to a hundred bass among us, too—all but three or four of them eight inches long. A different ecosystem, certainly, but no small river can take that kind of pressure.

The Fish Commission, apparently out of a concern that fishermen behave with decorum, has decreed that no more than six fish be kept on any one stringer; if you and I go out together, and if you catch six and I catch four, two under our combined limit; if nevertheless we raise them high at the dock all together, addicted to display as we evidently are, we could be in big trouble. The thought of a stringer like that stirs the reptilian brain. And here's an image more primitive yet, from a trip a few years ago. Some indistinct something, whitish, floating in one of the quiet reaches. Fish—putrefying fish, four bass on a stringer lost from a boat. The next time we went down they were still there.

We're not above counting ourselves rich because we've achieved the Fish Commission's limit—but that's just mind-static, and at some level we both know it. We fish to the limit of the day, of the river, of heart's desire.

We're too rich right now to care about casting for awhile. Jeremy says, "Check out the carp pool?"

"Let's do it."

You see carp cruising anywhere the water's not too fast; because they're plant-eaters, though, they tend to hang out in silt-bottomed pools and backwaters. Once they grow to a few pounds, too big for eagles, mink, raccoons, the biggest bass, they live a peaceful life. A big muskie can eat a ten-pound carp—but in this river, that would be a misadventure comparable to our canoe being sunk by a meteor. Being a perfect carp is easy.

The near edge of the carp pool is marked by a tangle of branches sticking out; against the shore, for the past month this summer, is lodged a bathroom-sized mat of cornstalks cut by muskrats. In between lies twenty feet or so of open water, clear, eight or ten feet deep, sand-bottomed. I ease the canoe along with just a touch of the paddle, striving to imitate a drifting log or a Nile crocodile—though the carp are in no danger. There they are, five of them—four in the five- to ten-pound range, the other, a fish we know—

"My God."

"Moby Carp."

It is, old Moby and no other. On a scale—but to be hoisted ignominiously into the air to satisfy curiosity is not his fate—he might weigh twenty pounds. In this little pocket of water he's simply outlandish, like a five-hundred-pound Sumo wrestler. Once Jeremy attempted to catch him—using a three-ounce bass rod rigged with six-pound-test line—by dangling a hook baited with corn in front of his nose. Naturally Moby ignored it. Bass, fast-swimming go-getters with high oxygen demands, go dormant for half the year (and a long, long six months it is). Moby is essentially dormant at all times. His energy expenditure is well off the low end of the human scale—*lazy bum* doesn't begin to describe it—and his metabolism about that of a hibernating frog. He resembles a master of Zen, one who can reduce his breathing and heart rate to near absolute zero. He approaches pure being.

Just back upstream is a good place to land for a snack and a swim, a sandy maple-shaded bank. Once in awhile, going by the fire ring, someone picnics here. Once as I was going down alone, well out toward the island, I spied a couple of motorboats pulled up, then four young fellows taking their ease on shore, then smelled, wafting across the channel, the sweet scent of cannabis. I was tempted, though not very, to play the crotchety elder and holler across: "You mean you can't get high on life? *Here?*" Today we have it to ourselves, as we've had the whole river since our encounter with the wading fisherman. (Who didn't, even by his own claim, catch anything like what Jeremy caught.) I'm ready to lay my head back on my boat cushion and close my eyes for a minute or two. I do. By the time I open them again, Jeremy, who's brought his swim mask and snorkel, is in the water. He sneaks heron-like along the verge to the muskrat mat, submerges, and disappears underneath it. I can't see the end of the snorkel poking up, though, as a minute turns to five, it must be. I linger on in the shade, feeling delectably ancient—I *could* be out there in the water, seeing whatever's to be seen, but I don't need to. My son is doing it. And here he comes now, with news:

"There must be thirty rock bass under there!"

A rock bass is a spiny panfish, red-eyed and hand-sized; we've caught them on our bass lures, but not so often lately. Nice to know they're still around.

"Cool."

"Yeah."

Jeremy eyes the tackle box, and I know what he's thinking—if he tied a little jig onto a piece of line and went back out there, he might catch one of those guys. Lunker bass are all very well, but childhood instinct runs strong. The boats can run out over the horizon on their quests for the great white something or other, yet there are fish worth rapt attention right *here,* right under the dock. Today he decides against it. Another day, maybe, which is one more joy of fishing home waters. There's always another day.

On down, and soon we reach, nearly opposite the downstream end of the large island, a narrow channel leading into what we call the Catfish Hole. This is yet another timber-choked backwater, tucked in behind a substantial gravel bar, which in seven or eight years has yielded two catfish. Blue cats, channel cats as their name suggests, actually tend to seek moving water—but it just has that look. That stagnant, fecund *southern* look, suggestive to the northern eye of water moccasins, alligators, snapping turtles—and big fish. Largemouth bass with mouths like saucers, catfish out of old, wild Mississippi legend. In sober actuality we've seen beaver in there, lots of herons, those two catfish, and I missed a strike from a nice bass the very first day we, Keith and I, fished the river. The last of four strikes, and I've wondered, since: suppose we'd raised one fish. Or two. How many were required for intimation to sink its hook? On how many bounteous home rivers do we never journey?

Today the water's too low to get in easily. We stay outside, drift the flat below the island—featureless water two or three feet deep where we raise something more often than not. And Jeremy does, a powerful fifteen-incher.

"Want to work up the other side of the island?" I ask.

"Your call." Traditionally, the call of whoever's had less luck. If this were a fishing tournament Jeremy would have won it, true enough, but I've had all the luck any man could want today. Besides, I'm still not sure about the sky.

"Head on down, then?"

"Sure."

Now picture us, if you can, for some hours hovering in another dimension as the river and the day flow on around us. Having started at first light from the landing at Montoursville, we've meandered along at a mile an hour or less—but the river flows one way, and we're still going to reach Muncy, eight miles below, by two or three o'clock. Picture us withdrawn from time for five hours, then, which makes it close to seven o'clock now as we reappear, the mellowest time of the day. The sun is still high. Prime evening bass fishing ahead, then, achieved by the kind of legerdemain which goes into those last-week-next-week fishing resort calendars? Not quite. By seven o'clock, often earlier, the bass on this river stop biting. I fished surface lures in the prime evening hours for years, simply because all my experience with bass in Minnesota told me to—nothing. These fish don't seek structure. They don't feed in the evening. What else? They're enigmatic, alien and familiar, wild as God.

"Getting a little late," I say. "I expect we've caught what we're going to catch. And if it's going to storm, I'd just as soon beat it down."

"Let's go."

eight
Last Cast

One day a fish bit late. I'd gone out with Ron in the early afternoon, after a summer class he was teaching ended, and by the time we got down to the Muncy Bridge, the lights were on. Seven lights across the span that reveal themselves, as you round the last bend, from left to right, one by one. Just above the bridge, between the second and third abutments from the right as you look downstream, is a spot which looks to the human eye like any other—a gentle flow over sandstone three or four feet down—but which, some years, has magnetized fish. Last chance at the end of hungry trips—one strike, with luck, for whoever's in most need. I can't remember what we'd caught on this particular day—something, enough—for all trips with Ron, a man of great good humor, are good ones. On toward 8:30, anyway, the river growing dusky, I threw my surface plug into this hole and something hit it. Something that with my light rod I simply couldn't move. It held on, held on until I thought it must be not a bass at all, but a big catfish. A bottom feeder rising to the surface would be strange, but it's happened to us twice: Jeremy caught one that way in the evening when we'd actually gone out catfishing but gotten skunked—except for a snapping turtle—on our stinky bait, and I had one rise out of deep water in broad daylight. This fish, though, finally jumped—a bass after all, a hell of a big one. It looked so massive in the net that I thought it must be twenty inches at least, instead of eighteen and a half by tape. Four pounds or close. And that, for I was not remotely tempted to throw my lure out again, was my best last cast on the river.

I think of the last cast I will ever throw into this sweet water. Most likely nothing will come to it. Most likely I won't recognize it—the end of summer merely, the year will turn as it does, spring will come as it must—and I used to think I wouldn't want to. The ends of the Pine Terrace trips were, for a boy of eleven and twelve and thirteen, small deaths. The morning we had to go, we'd walk the path to Beaver Lake one last time, cast around it once. The fish might bite or not, but we could see the end coming the whole way around. An hour, one circuit of the minute hand around the dial, here was the landing. Last cast. One more for luck. See you next year? With school between? Like hearing in Sunday school that if you live a good life you need fear nothing, for you'll surely go to Heaven.

My parents, now close to ninety years old, visit us for a week each summer. Their age has closed much of the world off from them; each year our walks in the woods grow slower and shorter. For a trip down the river, though, a greatly anticipated ritual, a passenger need only sit in the boat. I'd take them down in the johnboat separately, Jeremy along with my father for the fishing; my mother and I alone, as Jeremy found it hard to know what to say. (Nothing at all, of course, beyond reserved replies to grandmotherly questions, but still—how, dressed up for Sunday, can you dive naked into the day?) My father, who still fishes for bluegill in Kansas ponds and still eats them, casts with less than the vigor of thirty years ago—or even ten—but all you have to do is land the plug on the water, and he gets his share of strikes. Only his reflexes are gone, so he misses most of them. He has, though, big fish luck—call it luck or being in tune with something. For three years in a row he hooked bass, and landed two of them, of eighteen inches or more. This past year, when I asked him which day he wanted to go down, he told me a trip that long would be too tiring. Which is one of those moments that raise the hair on the back of your neck. Then you settle into a sort of perpetual yellow alert. Everyone with aging parents knows about this: that maybe next year, maybe tomorrow or the next minute, the phone is going to ring.

A couple of miles up from Montoursville is another landing, one we don't ordinarily use—the river up that way is wide and slow, not bassy. From the mouth of the Loyalsock Creek, though—and sometimes when we want a long day we launch from there—on down to the regular landing we've had decent luck. Prospects for actually catching something, anyway, seemed a little beside the point. I offered my father this short trip, aware all the while of the lovely stretches downstream which he would never again see, and he allowed that that would be about right. Never see. What line in all the classic literature can freeze your blood like that one word, five times repeated, as Lear holds his lifeless daughter in his arms? We went out, Jeremy having sensibly declined; the upstream stretch of water was what it was. Not much sign of anything. Then, still upstream from the creek mouth, we came to a weedbed where at times we've caught fish—the utmost reach of our quotidian journeyings. Off the bottom of this weedbed my father hooked a fish—it hooked itself—which fought hard for several minutes. Anxious minutes for me, like the time when Jeremy hooked his first big one; though my father would have said, had it gotten off, "It's okay. I've caught lots of fish." Yes, but . . . I was not prepared for any of those to be his last fish. Last big one. The fish did not get off. It measured seventeen inches, lean and powerful, a beauty. That was what we caught that day. And I do not at this moment know if my father has cast his last cast into the bounteous waters of the Susquehanna River.

My mother's first cast did not land in the water. As a girl she used to go with an aunt and cousins on extended summer trips to Rock Island, Tennessee, a hundred miles or so from her home in Nashville. The water she was aiming at was the Collins River; what she was aiming at it, having walked down to the bank with a borrowed cane pole, was a hook baited with a piece of ripe meat. She slung it out in a convoluted arc which ended with the hook buried in her thumb, and then had to walk back up and find somebody to cut it out. By some oddity she did not develop gangrene. I like to think that if she *had* landed her bait in that southern river, she'd have pulled out a fine catfish.

Undeterred by that shaky start, she took up fishing again when she married a fisherman, and on outings to Canadian lakes with her husband and father-in-law she caught fish. No record of first fish or first big fish remains, but several were notable: a sixteen-pound lake trout, trolled up from the depths on a wire line; at Pine Terrace the biggest bass, that five-pound monster, the biggest pike, weighing over seven pounds, and the biggest walleye, five and a half; and from the headwaters of the Mackenzie River, during the Brabant Island week, pike weighing at least fourteen. All this despite the tendency of her casts to rise almost straight into the air in a pop-fly arc and land a few yards from the boat. My casts, by the time I reached my mid-teens, flew out like line drives. There was, I concluded, in the fishing world no justice.

How many years ago and in what water my mother last fished is lost—a trivial detail, for it was always the experience of being on or beside the water that counted for her. A year ago last July we went out on the Susquehanna together—I set up a camp chair in the johnboat to rest her creaky back—and this was the day we had: it was warm but not hot, bright, no threat of rain. Ducks and geese, herons and kingfishers everywhere. We got down in five-and-half hours in low water without hitting anything. And the bass were feeding like lunatics. I caught ten all by myself, seven of them big ones—sixteen inches and up—and one, at twenty inches and over four and a quarter pounds, the biggest I've ever caught anywhere. Had I put the six biggest on a stringer and carried them to the office of the *Sun-Gazette,* I'd have had my picture in the paper. It was, almost certainly, the best day of bass fishing that anyone has ever had on that stretch of water. My mother liked it. She liked it a lot, especially that I was putting them back. The following summer the water was higher, the fishing slower, the river eternally lovely. My mother had slowed down in the intervening year, and at moments of stress her mind wandered. When I asked about a river trip she informed me—matter-of-factly, almost as if I ought to have known—that it would be too tiring. Last cast was last year. The end had come when I wasn't looking.

Now Jeremy and I meander on down toward our own last cast of the day. At the bottom of the flat is a fast shallow riffle full of low-water ambushes; we put another dent or two in the canoe, then get out and walk.

A little way down on the left is a sandstone ledge, fifty yards wide by three hundred or so long. The bank behind it, an enigmatic artifact—a retaining wall of squared stones, laid dry, rising fifteen to twenty feet to the level forest floor. No one I've asked has known its history or purpose; it may have had something to do with those three-hundred-foot lumber rafts, but then why, along the whole two-hundred-mile route, reinforce this one bend? The ledge, when exposed as it is today, makes the river look tidal. The shore birds here are sandpipers. Shallow pools form which, in the afternoon sunlight, get warmer than blood. The water off the ledge runs as deep as any along our route, maybe ten or twelve feet, and the *we* who did *not* step out of the river of time for five hours, who therefore have arrived at 2:30 in the afternoon, stop here to swim.

A long reach. We paddle steadily, not in a rush but not dawdling either. Thunder rumbles a long way back up the river, eight or ten seconds still between flicker and boom as we approach the bridge. So, a hundred yards short of it, we settle back into the drift and cast again. Two years ago my father lost a huge bass here, maybe as much as twenty inches. It was okay, he said. He'd caught lots of fish.

This evening, as the sky turns to pewter and the first bats swoop over the water, the fish hold true to their ways. Nothing and nothing again—we've caught what we're going to. Which in a sense makes the honor of throwing the last cast into the bridge hole an empty one, but still. I lean the rod tip back over my shoulder . . . .

I would like to know, of the last cast I will ever cast into this river, that that is what it is. I'd aim it at eternity. Which seems, as the rod tenses and for an instant stills, the proper destination for the last cast of this day's journey. I've heard there are big ones out that way.

Afterword

The johnboat, twelve feet long and weighing a hundred-and-five pounds, perches neatly on top of my '95 Dodge Caravan. I've driven the van to the Montoursville landing, backed it halfway down the ramp, around ten o'clock on the morning of September 10, 2001. In twenty-four hours or so the World Trade Center will fall down, but here and now it's a mellow day—b rilliantly sunlit, summer still. The routine and simple way of offloading the boat unaided is this: First, release the cam buckles, draw the loosened straps off the boat, and toss them into the van through the open window. Second, with one foot braced on the back bumper, grasp the boat by its two stern handles and walk it back until only the bow rests on the rear carrier bar. Third, lower the stern to the ramp. Fourth, raise the bow of the boat, now leaning against the back of the van at a forty-five-degree angle, cautiously to the vertical. Fifth and finally, by walking backwards ease the bow down, such that if I've positioned the van correctly, the front of the boat and my feet are actually in the edge of the river. But before I get to that point, the boat still upright, I hear a tremulous voice right behind me: "Honey, can I help?" It is that of my mother—eighty-seven years old, five feet tall, weighing a pound or two more than the boat, constitutionally inattentive, nearly blind, and wobbly with grief, for the errand we are about is to scatter my father's ashes in the West Branch. I lean the boat back up against the van and walk her over to the grass verge. Yes. She can help by standing out of the way, so I don't drop the boat on her.

In December 2000, my parents quite casually decided to move to Pennsylvania from their half-century home in Kansas. At the beginning of June I flew out and drove them east. So there was my father and there was the river, and it was fishing season. Only he had moved also into the country of the very old. Originally six feet tall, he was now so stooped that I could see the top of his head at eye level. He shuffled, set the heel of one foot down barely past the toe of the other. Mowing the lawn, an ordeal from which we could not dissuade him, laid him flat down for hours. We'd have to get out on the river when he was rested up from the move, I said, and he agreed that we would. But he grew no stronger and said nothing about it, so we went blueberry picking instead. Wild high-bush blueberries—no stooping or kneeling for an old man—growing on a wooded lakeshore. While we picked, my mother sat in her folding chair beneath an ancient white pine, meditating and praying.

The fishing on the West Branch was slower that summer, but not slow enough to matter. I went out with Jeremy, with friends, and alone. I was alone in the johnboat one day, well downstream below the ledge, when there came a big whack and a big jolt. Big fish, too—nineteen or twenty inches and as close to flat black as a smallmouth can get: an exotic risen from some deeper place than I knew of. Eleven big fish I'd lost in my life, and remembered every one. If this one got off it would be the twelfth. It did, on a second jump close to the boat, and it was. One more swimmer in the River of Lost Dreams.

On September 4, 2001, I got home from my evening teaching job around nine o'clock, just about the time my father's first heart attack was starting. He had fierce radiating chest pains that he fobbed off as indigestion—done in by an off-color meatloaf. So it was not until eleven, my wife and I sleeping, that he allowed my mother to call us. They had never heard of 9-1-1. The ambulance and I arrived together in less than ten minutes, and he was stabilized in the Williamsport Hospital Emergency Room and admitted to the Intensive Care Unit late that night. There, seemingly, he did so well that he was moved to a private room in the medical wing the following afternoon. Two days later, around five o'clock, my mother and I were there for what we assumed would be a routine visit. I was planning to take Jeremy to a Williamsport Crosscutters baseball game that evening. But within a few minutes I saw my father's face twist, and this time the nitroglycerine did nothing. He went into ventricular fibrillation, what the medical pros call V-fib, and in less than two hours he was gone.

Some forty hours later, the funeral home I arbitrarily engaged reduced him from a hundred twenty-five pounds—he was gaunt in his old age—to a volume of ashes which would have fit into a gallon milk jug. They came to us in a heavy-gauge plastic bag, itself enclosed in a shiny reddish-brown pasteboard box: industry standard, I take it, for it was a larger replica of the boxes in which we'd received the cremated remains—the cremains, in funerary jargon—of our cats. Fourteen hundred-some-odd dollars for a direct cremation, memorial service to be held later at the family's convenience. We held it in the two-hundred-year-old stone Quaker Meeting House in Pennsdale, in the manner of Friends—silent and vocal witnessing. To the twenty or so assembled, only six of whom had known him, I read his poems about the snapping turtle and the dogfish.

My mother and I were both aware, though in anxious moments she asked to be reminded, that the ashes were not her husband and my father. The shrinkage had occurred when his spirit departed. So it was simply a matter of disposing of them respectfully in a natural setting, in accordance with his wishes. "Natural setting" to me meant the river; my mother readily agreed. Only where and in what manner in the river? I pictured doing it in the course of a fishing trip, in the jolly spirit of an Irish wake. That's how Jeremy is to dispose of my mortal remains, ultimately: first, catch a bass; try and make it a nice one. Restore the bass to the water. With neither more nor less ceremony, deep-six the ashes. Unless of course the fish aren't biting that day, in which case any riffle will do. You do what you can.

What I can do in this case is severely limited, because my mother wants to participate directly. As why shouldn't she? Which leaves us three options I can think of:

Simplify: leave the boat home; dump the ashes into the shallows off the landing. Only there are likely to be witnesses; moreover, this setting is marginally natural. I've cleaned it of more than one potato chip bag, with a gingerly toe edged out into the current a putrid carp or two. Maybe not.

So use the boat, but make it easy: row out into the middle of the landing pool and drop the ashes into the water. The still water, a scenario not quite to my liking. Not that I suppose the ashes will make it to the Chesapeake, but even so, that initial surge *toward* the ocean speaks to me somehow. Which leaves the problematical, given the age of my passenger the actually risky, approach:

Row all the way across to the head of the riffle, the one that flows down the far side of the first island. Try to find a deep enough spot—with no empirical definition of *deep enough*—which is, simultaneously, *shallow* enough so that I don't lose the boat. Not *lose* as in *never see again*. (Like my glasses, watch, paddle, rod, and Jeremy's cap.) No, lose as in a rowboat with my mother in it and me not in it, sliding down the chute toward the rock on which we foundered a couple of summers ago. And that is why, as we set out across the landing pool on the brilliant morning of September 10, twenty-four hours before the death of the Trade Center, my mother is wearing a personal flotation device. I have plenty of time to think—about some people who set out in a small plane to scatter ashes over the ocean, launched them into the slipstream which spat them right back into the cabin. Such ashes apparently have a certain *stickiness* . . .

How could anyone possibly be that blank?

My mother has been thinking also, about the possibility that an ash or two might not get scattered and so end up in the landfill. Could we leave the bag itself—the heavy-gauge plastic, non-biodegradable bag—in the river? No, we could not. But I promise to turn it inside out and submerge it. Then she thinks we should *both* upend it into the water, a tricky little sonata for four hands. So much for my notion of grounding the boat in the shallows and wading, all by myself, twenty yards to the head of the chute. So . . . .

Here we are. I bump the bow into a rock and scramble out, bracing the boat amidships with my legs. The water is shin-deep—twelve or fourteen inches, nothing like enough. I know that absolutely, but there's nothing else for it. I raise the bag, the heft of it just that of a big West Branch smallmouth, and undo the twist tie. Four hands. Over it goes. Some of the ashes float and form a long gray slick. Some sink and form a long gray smear. And any residual memory of what this is supposed to be about sinks also. I think precisely this: *Oh, hell. I have polluted the river.*

And then I drag the boat back out into slightly deeper water, clamber aboard, and row us back to the landing. A big flock of mallards whistles by not thirty yards overhead; my mother can neither see nor hear them. A great blue heron poses picturesquely on a log; no point in mentioning it. All in all, it seems fortunate that those ashes are not, in any significant sense, Will Moses.

What emerges almost at once is that I don't want this to have been my last river journey until spring. So a few days later I go down one more time, alone in the johnboat with my familiar gear. Another nice day. The gray smear is still visible but greatly diminished, so it's all right: already, a long way upstream, the heavy water of March and April is building up. I catch a couple of nice fish, send them back home, and go home myself. It feels like closing up a summerhouse for the season. Be safe. Be blessed. *See you next year.*

Ed Moses lives in Williamsport, Pennsylvania, and continues to fish the West Branch of the Susquehanna River. The river remains as bountiful as ever.